AQA Funct English

Assessment Book

Imelda Pilgrim

Peter Buckroyd

Nelson Thornes

Published in 2008 by:
Nelson Thornes Ltd
Delta Place
27 Bath Road
CHELTENHAM
GL53 7TH
United Kingdom

08 09 10 11 12 / 10 9 8 7 6 5 4 3 2 1

A catalogue record for this book is available from the British Library

ISBN 978 1 4085 0242 6

Cover photograph © Nelson Thornes Ltd
Page make-up by Viners Wood Associates

Printed and bound in Spain by Graphycems

Acknowledgements

Text
AQA materials reprinted with kind permission of AQA
QCA materials reprinted with permission of QCA
P8: ActionAid advert 'One day she'll make you proud' (c) ActionAid. Reproduced with permission.
P11: ActionAid text 'The children who don't exist' © ActionAid. Reproduced with permission.
P14: Extract from NHS Organ Donation leaflet, © NHS, leaflet number 90142/UKT September 2004. Reproduced with
    permission of UK Transplant.
P16: Extract from *So you think your home is safe?* leaflet by the Electrical Safety Council, www.electricalsafetycouncil.
    org.uk, 18 Buckingham Gate, SW1E 6LB, 0870 040 0561, leaflet number V2Nov06, pages 16 to 17. Reproduced
    with permission.
P18: Extracts from their *Summer Sun 2008* brochure reproduced by kind permission of Olympic Holidays.
P20: Embsay Station and Bolton Abbey. Reprinted with permission of Embsay Station.
P22: Zion Arts Centre leaflet. Reprinted with permission.
P24: Motoring extract from www.direct.gov.uk. Reproduced with permission. Crown Copyright © 2008.
P26: Extract from YHA Discover magazine, Spring/Summer 08, www.yha.org.uk. Reproduced with permission.
P28: National Trust letter © National Trust. Reprinted with kind permission.
P30: 'How long are you here for' leaflet reprinted with permission of Road Peace.
P32: Work & Study text from DFES Leaflet. Booklet reference PRE1607, © Crown Copyright 2006, produced for
    DFES September 2006.
P34: Go Further text and map © Nexus. Reprinted with permission.
P36: edited extract from www.animal-job.co.uk/Zoo-Keeper. Reproduced with permission.
P38: English Heritage Education 2007. Reprinted with kind permission.
P40: Extract from Greater Manchester Waste Disposal Authority leaflet 'A cleaner, greener place to be'. Reprinted
    with permission.
P42: Mamma Mia poster produced by little star. God of Carnage poster produced by David Pugh and Dafydd Rogers.
    Surrounding text courtesy of Delfont Mackintosh Theatres.
P44: Advertisement for Scotts of Stow stainless steel thermal cafetière reproduced with permission.

Photos
P8: Sofi image – © Liba Taylor/ActionAid.
P11: Photograph of Domina © Tom Pietrasik/ActionAid.
P18: Photo from their *Summer Sun 2008* brochure reproduced by kind permission of Olympic Holidays.
P20: © Embsay Station and © the Chatsworth Settlement Trustees, Bolton Abbey.
P24: Driving test (6354439) © iStock.com.
P26: Big Ben and street scene (2234370) © iStock.com; Buckingham palace (4961908) © iStock.com;
    Cyclist by the Thames (3571333) © iStock.com.
P32: Young man in black clothes (2405830) © iStock.com; Helicopter (4322695) © iStock.com.

Contents

Functional English assessment

The three core elements in English are:

- Reading
- Writing
- Speaking and Listening.

The Functional English qualification is designed to improve and test your competency in each of these three elements. This is to ensure that you have a level of competence in English that will enable you to succeed in further education and in the workplace.

Levels

There are five levels of achievement in Functional English:

Entry 1	Entry 2	Entry 3	Level 1	Level 2

In order to gain a Functional English qualification, you need to achieve Level 1 or Level 2. To do this you will need to take and pass externally set tests in Reading and Writing. Your Speaking and Listening will be assessed by your teacher. Your Functional English achievements will then form part of your Diploma and from 2010 onwards, will help decide your grade in GCSE English. This is explained in the boxes below.

FUNCTIONAL ENGLISH AND DIPLOMAS

- You will need a Functional English pass to be awarded a Diploma in any subject.
- To gain a Level 1 Diploma, you will need a Level 1 in Reading, Writing *and* Speaking and Listening.
- To gain a Level 2 Diploma, you will need a Level 2 in all three elements.

FUNCTIONAL ENGLISH AND GCSE ENGLISH

- From 2010 onwards you will need a Functional English Level 2 in Reading, Writing *and* Speaking and Listening in order to gain a Grade C or above in GCSE English.

What do I need to do to pass?

The boxes on page 5 describe what you need to do in order to gain a Level 1 or Level 2 in the three main elements and how you will be assessed. This book will guide you through all the assessments you will face, in 'sample' assessments with lots of support. You will also be offered 'practice' assessments so that you can have a go at answering under exam style conditions. Answers to the Reading assessments can be found at the back of the book.

Unit 1 Reading

What do I need to do?

Level 1:
Read and understand a range of texts.

Level 2:
Compare, select, read and understand texts and use them to gather information, ideas, arguments and opinions.

How am I assessed?

- You will take a timed test in which you read a number of source texts and answer 6 multiple-choice questions about each of them.

- If you take the Level 1 Reading test it will last for 45 minutes and you will have to answer 12 questions.

- The combined Level 1 *and* Level 2 Reading test will last for one hour and you will have to answer 36 questions.

- You will be allowed to use a dictionary in the exam.

Unit 2 Writing

What do I need to do?

Level 1:
Write documents to communicate information, ideas and opinions using formats and styles suitable for their purpose and audience.

Level 2:
Write documents, including extended writing pieces, communicating information, ideas and opinions, effectively and persuasively.

How am I assessed?

- You will take a timed test in which you will complete a writing task.

- If you take the Level 1 Writing test it will last for 45 minutes and you will have to write to inform.

- The combined Level 1 *and* Level 2 Writing test will last for one hour and you will have to inform and persuade.

- You will be allowed to use a dictionary in the exam.

Unit 3 Speaking and Listening

What do I need to do?

Level 1:
Take full part in formal and informal discussions/exchanges.

Level 2:
Make a range of contributions to discussions and make effective presentations.

How am I assessed?

- You will take part in a range of Speaking and Listening activities and your performance will be assessed by your teacher.

Unit 1 Reading

To determine your level in Reading you will take a timed test. In this test, you will read a number of different types of source text and answer multiple-choice questions on them. This means that you will be given four possible answers to each question from which you have to choose the correct one. You may use a dictionary in the test.

The different levels

For Reading Level 1 you need to:
- identify the main points and ideas and how they are presented in different texts
- understand texts in detail
- read and understand texts and take appropriate action.

For Reading Level 2 you need to:
- select and use different types of text to obtain relevant information
- read and summarise succinctly information/ ideas from different sources
- identify the purposes of texts and comment on how effectively meaning is conveyed
- detect point of view, implicit meaning and/or bias
- read and actively respond to different texts.

Tackling multiple-choice questions

In your Reading test you will read different texts (called 'Sources') and answer multiple-choice questions on them.

- You must base your answers only on each text and what you learn from it.
- There is only one correct answer to each question.
- When you have read the questions and the notes, choose your answer. Then write down the question number and your choice of letter beside it.

The exam paper

Look at page 7 – this shows you what the front page of a Reading paper will look like. Always read the front page carefully before starting to answer, making sure you understand exactly what is required of you. The annotations given on page 7 will help you to do this.

Practice

Sample papers with notes to help you answer the questions correctly are provided on pages 8-13, while further exam-style practice papers without notes are given on pages 14-45. Please note that the Level 1 text and questions on the Level 1/2 paper would normally be exactly the same as on the Level 1 paper. In this book, however, we have provided different texts and questions to give you as much practice as possible.

Use the 'Top tips' on page 72 to help you complete the activities, to renew your learning, and to revise before the test.

Functional Skills
January 2008

000000
Level 1

AQA

ASSESSMENT AND
QUALIFICATIONS
ALLIANCE

ENGLISH
Multiple Choice Reading
January 2008

This is the test you are taking.

Unit 0 000000 – Level 1

For this paper you must have:
- An objective test answer sheet
- A black ball-point pen

Make sure you have everything you need.

Specimen Paper

Time allowed: 45 minutes

Make a note of how long you have got – you need to allow time to answer all the questions.

Always read the instructions carefully.

Instructions

- Use a ball-point pen for recording your answers to Questions A1 to B12 on your objective test answer sheet.
- Answer **all** questions.
- For each question there are several alternative responses. When you have selected the response which you think is the best to answer the question, mark this response on your answer sheet.
- Mark all responses as instructed on your answer sheet. If you wish to change your answer, follow the instructions on your answer sheet.
- Do all rough work in this book, **not** on your answer sheet.
- You may use a dictionary if you wish.

Do exactly what the instructions tell you – you will lose valuable marks if you miss a question or put the right answer in the wrong place.

Make sure you have everything you need.

Information
- The maximum mark for this paper is 12.
- Each question has only **one** right answer.

Here is more useful information to help you do your best.

© AQA

7

Source A Level 1

One day she'll make you proud

Photograph and case study for representation only. Liba Taylor/ActionAid

Please send me further details about sponsoring a child, or call 01460 23 80 80.

I'm interested in sponsoring in: ☐ Africa ☐ Asia ☐ Where need is greatest

Mr/Mrs/Miss/Ms
_____

Address
_____

Postcode
_____

Tel (Day) _____ (Eve) _____

200195

I can't sponsor a child now, but enclose a gift of:
☐ £200 ☐ £100 ☐ £50 ☐ £25 ☐ £_____

ActionAid and our subsidiaries may contact you with more information about our activities. If you do not wish to receive this information, please tick this box ☐.

Make cheques/POs payable to ActionAid, and send to:
ActionAid
FREEPOST BS4868
CHARD, TA20 1BR
www.actionaid.org.uk

act!onaid

Child Sponsorship
Registered Charity No. 274467

Officially, seven year old Sofi doesn't exist. She was born in one of Kolkata's poorest slums – and because her birth is not registered, she has no right to schooling or medical care. She spends her days picking rags to make a few rupees for her family. Almost every week the police evict her family, beating them and breaking their few possessions.

But for a couple of hours a day, Sofi attends a club where she's learning to read and write. She studies hard because she wants to be a policewoman – a policewoman who is kind to poor families like hers.

Wouldn't you be proud of a child like Sofi? By sponsoring a child through ActionAid, you could be.

As a child sponsor, you can help a whole community access the safe, clean water, health care and education they need to build a brighter future. You'll receive a photograph and personal messages from the child and updates from the local field workers.

Please sponsor a child like Sofi today.

© ActionAid

Sample Reading assessment Level 1

Read the text on page 8, Source A, an advert for the charity ActionAid. Then try the multiple choice questions below. The notes show you what skills are being targeted in the questions and give advice on how to answer them. The questions target Level 1 skills. There are 8 questions in total; in the exam you will only face 6 on each source text.

> **NOTES**
>
> Questions A1 and A2 are asking you to identify the main points and ideas of the advert, Source A. Read each question and each option carefully. You need to read the whole text closely and not just put down the first thing you think of. For example, in Question A1 option A uses a word from the heading. Some students would immediately think this was the correct answer and not bother to read the rest of the source text and think carefully. They would get the answer wrong!

A1 The writer of this advert wants the reader to

  A   feel proud of Sofi
  B   feel sorry for Sofi
  C   sponsor a child like Sofi
  D   find out more about Kolkata

A2 Sofi has no right to schooling or medical care because

  A   Sofi doesn't exist
  B   she was born in one of Kolkata's poorest slums
  C   her birth is not registered
  D   almost every week the police evict her family

> **NOTES**
>
> Questions A3 and A4 are asking you to think about how the main points and ideas are presented and organised. Read each question and each option carefully. You might be able to eliminate some of the options fairly quickly. For example, in Question A3 option B says 'The headline tells you about Sofi's life'. As the headline is 'One day she'll make you proud', this is clearly not correct. Once you have ruled out the options you are sure are not correct, go back to the text and check out the others.

A3 Which of the following statements is true?

  A   The first two paragraphs describe Sofi's life.
  B   The headline tells you about Sofi's life.
  C   Sofi's life is not described.
  D   The picture shows Sofi's family

A4 Which of the following statements is true?

  A   The written text is all about Sofi.
  B   The picture shows you where Sofi lives.
  C   The picture shows that Sofi is a sad child.
  D   The reply form does not refer to Sofi

A5   Sofi wants to be a policewoman who

A   earns more money
B   studies hard
C   evict families
D   is kind to poor families like hers

A6   As a child sponsor you will

A   stop the police brutality
B   help to open more clubs
C   receive a photograph of local field workers
D   receive personal messages from the child

A7   If you wanted to sponsor a child like Sofi you would

A   send money to Sofi
B   visit Kolkata
C   complete the reply form or telephone the number given
D   make a cheque out to ActionAid

A8   If you fill in and post the reply form you

A   are asking for information or making a donation
B   are promising to make a payment to the Post Office
C   are agreeing to receive a phone call about Sofi
D   are agreeing to sponsor a child like Sofi

Checkpoint

a Check your answers with another student.

b Where you have different answers, re-read the advert and decide who is correct.

c When you are happy with your answers, check them against the list of correct answers on page 75. If you were incorrect on any of them, take another look and try to work out where you went wrong.

d What can you do to improve your answers in future? Set yourself a target for improving your next attempt. For example, 'Read the detail of the text more carefully.'

Sample Reading assessment Level 2

Read the text below, source B, an extract about children's lives in Kolkata (Calcutta). Then try the multiple-choice questions that follow it. The questions target Level 2 skills. To achieve Level 2 you are expected to give answers to questions based on more complex texts. You are also expected to be able to compare texts, therefore for questions B14 and B15 you need to use Source A, on page 8, as well as Source B below. There are 7 questions in total. In the exam there will be 5 questions on each source text and 4 comparison questions in total.

Source B Level 2

The children who don't exist

It is early evening in downtown Kolkata (formerly Calcutta), and rush-hour traffic starts to build. On this busy stretch of Diamond Harbour Street, lined with offices and shopping malls, taxis and brightly coloured buses pile up at the lights, honking furiously. On the pavements, suited commuters hurry past. Some talk into phones, some hail taxis – but few spare a glance for the small girl sitting cross-legged on the filthy paving stones. Nor is she paying much attention to them; she is too busy peering at a textbook balanced on her knee. Beside her, just beyond the trampling feet, is a battered schoolbag containing more books and paper and pens. This is Domina Khartun and, amid the chaos, she is trying to do her homework.

Domina is ten years old. Like dozens of other children in this stretch of street, she was born here and has called the pavements home her whole life. But unlike the other kids here, Domina has one crucial advantage: technically, she exists.

The reason is simple: she has a birth certificate, a vital piece of paper that means the state acknowledges her as an official citizen. The problem for the homeless population in Kolkata is that, to acquire a birth certificate, it is necessary to provide a residential address. Those born on the pavements cannot do this. The only reason Domina is different is that when she was born, her mother was working in an office where she had made friends with an official, who offered her an address with which to register the baby.

That simple gesture changed Domina's life forever. With a birth certificate, she has been

Ten-year-old Domina has no choice but to do her homework on the streets.

" *WE ALL SLEEP TOGETHER ON THE STREET, WHICH HELPS... BUT IT'S STILL NOT SAFE.* "
MARIAN

able to enrol at school. As she grows older, it will entitle her to a ration card and state assistance. She will be able to open a bank account and vote. With an education, she may be able to get a job and find somewhere permanent to live.

This one piece of paper represents hope not just for Domina but for the entire family, and they are doing all they can to ensure it is not squandered. Her mother, Marian, is a kitchen-hand and her father is one of the city's 18,000 rickshaw pullers. They work long hours to scrape together the 270 rupees (£3.20) per year for Domina's school fees, and to buy books and some clothes so she can go to school in something more than rags. Every day, they walk her to school, and when her day finishes, they collect her and bring her home to the Diamond Harbour pavement.

© ActionAid

Question B9 asks you to identify which statement best summarises the ideas in the whole text. To get this right you need to read the full text carefully, following the points the writer is making. When you have finished reading, you need to consider which statement best shows the connection between the different details in the text. For example, option A only refers to details from the first paragraph and therefore cannot be the correct answer.

B9   Which of the following best summarises the points made in the whole text?

    A   Domina does her homework on the pavement.
    B   Domina has a birth certificate.
    C   Having a birth certificate has made a big difference to Domina's life.
    D   Domina's family work hard to ensure she goes to school.

NOTES Question B10 asks you to identify the purpose of the text. To do this you need to think about what the writer has set out to do. It is not enough to simply identify a detail of the text. For example, the writer does describe Domina's family life, as suggested in option C. That is done only in the final paragraph; it is not the main purpose of the text.

B10   The main purpose of the text is to

    A   ask you for money to help Domina
    B   inform the reader about the importance of a birth certificate in Kolkata
    C   describe Domina's family life
    D   show you how hard Domina works

NOTES Question B11 asks you to comment on how effective meaning is conveyed to the reader. You need to consider the picture and caption and think about how they connect with the writing. For example, there is no mention of Domina having a brother in the passage so option D cannot be correct.

B11   The picture and caption are used effectively to

    A   illustrate the first paragraph
    B   show you two children on the streets
    C   present a picture of rush hour in Kolkata
    D   show you Domina with her brother

NOTES Question B12 asks you to think about what the writer is implying. You need to look beneath the surface details and work out what is suggested by them. Re-read the final paragraph and decide what the writer is suggesting through the range of details given.

B12   The final paragraph suggests that

    A   Domina will do well in the future
    B   her parents could work harder
    C   the school fees are too high
    D   the family's hope for the future depends on Domina being successful

NOTES

Question B13 is asking you about what might be an appropriate response to take to reading this text. All the options are possible responses but only one is an appropriate response. Think carefully about what you have read before identifying the correct option.

B13 An appropriate response to reading this text would be

A to recognise the unfairness of life in Kolkata
B to feel sorry for Domina
C to take a holiday in Kolkata
D to write to Domina

NOTES

Questions B14 and B15 are comparative questions. They are asking you to obtain relevant information from different types of text. In order to answer them correctly you will need to consider Source A, the advert, *and* Source B, the extract from an article. Whilst some of the options may be true of one text, only one is true of both texts. So, for example, whilst Source A does show that ActionAid is working to help children in Kolkata, no mention of ActionAid is made in Source B. Option D for question B14, therefore, cannot be the correct answer.

The following two questions refer to sources A and B.

B14 Both texts tell you that

A without a birth certificate, you have no right to schooling in Kolkata
B parents need to work hard to keep a child in school
C children in Kolkata need your help
D ActionAid is working to help children in Kolkata

B15 One similarity between Sources A and B is that

A they both want the reader to visit Kolkata
B they both promote ActionAid
C they both describe the life of a young girl
D they both ask for help

Checkpoint

a Check your answers with another student.
b Where you have different answers re-read the text(s) and decide who is correct.
c When you are happy with your answers, check them against the list of correct answers on page 75. If you were incorrect on any of them, take another look and try to work out where you went wrong.
d What can you do to improve your answers in future? Set yourself a target for improving your next attempt. For example, 'Make sure to read *both* texts closely when answering comparative questions.'

Practice Reading assessment 1 Level 1

Practise a Level 1 Reading assessment by completing the following paper. Read Source A below carefully, then answer the 6 questions that follow. Next read Source B and answer the following 6 questions. There is only one correct answer to each question. You have 45 minutes to complete all 12 questions. You may use a dictionary if you wish.

Source A Level 1

Give the gift of life

Transplants are one of the most miraculous achievements of modern medicine. But they depend entirely on the generosity of donors and their families who are willing to make this life-saving gift to others.

One donor can give life to several people and restore the sight of two more.

There is a critical shortage of organs and the gap between the number of organs donated and the number of people waiting for a transplant is increasing. Right now, more than 9,000 people in the UK need an organ transplant and every year around 400 people die while waiting.

The need for donors has never been greater. So why not sign up to life now? Leave the gift of life today.

What is organ donation?

Organ donation is the gift of an organ to help someone else who needs a transplant. Hundreds of people's lives are saved each year by the generosity of organ donors.

Organs that can be donated after death include the heart, lungs, kidneys, liver, pancreas and small bowel. Tissue such as skin, bone, heart valves and corneas can also be used to help others.

Doctors and nurses are committed to doing everything possible to save life and organ donation only takes place after a patient has died. Most donated organs come from people who die while on a ventilator in an intensive care unit, following a severe brain injury.

TEAR AND MOISTEN GLUED EDGE OPPOSITE

Leave someone a future

To decide whether or not you wish to give life to someone else after you have died is something very personal and it is important that everyone makes their own decision.

Even if you already carry a donor card you should join the NHS Organ Donor Register to ensure your wishes are recorded. Discuss your decision with those closest to you so they know your wishes should the time ever come.

By joining the register you are giving your agreement to your organs and tissue being used for transplantation to save or enhance the lives of others after your death.

Adding your name to the register will only take a few minutes of your time. But it could save someone else's life.

How to join the register

- **Call 0845 60 60 400**
- **Visit www.uktransplant.org.uk**
- **Fill in the attached form and return it to us.**

Thank you

© NHS

Each of **Questions A1** to **B12** is followed by four responses A, B, C and D. For each question select the best response. Write the question number and your choice of letter beside it.

Questions 1 to 6 refer to Source A

A1 The *main* purpose of this text is to

    A   tell the reader about the work of doctors and nurses

    B   criticise the success rate of organ donation

    C   persuade the reader to join the NHS Organ Donor Register

    D   tell the reader which organs can be donated

A2 Which of the following statements best describes how the detail in the text is organised?

    A   It starts by telling the reader where he/she should go to register as an organ donor.

    B   It gives information about organ donation before telling the reader about the Organ Donor Register.

    C   It gives information about organ donation after telling the reader about the Organ Donor Register.

    D   It tells you about organ donation but does not explain what the Organ Donor Register is.

A3 The writer informs you that

    A   doctors and nurses are responsible for raising awareness of the problem

    B   transplants have taken place since Roman times

    C   400 people need an organ transplant in the UK every year

    D   there are not enough organs donated to meet the need for transplants

A4 The writer also informs you that

    A   there are 9,000 people on the Organ Donor Register

    B   joining the Register could save someone's life

    C   they need to raise more money for organ donation

    D   your family is not allowed to help you make the decision

A5 According to the leaflet, if you already carry a donor card you should

    A   make sure your card is safe

    B   write to your MP about the situation

    C   still record your wishes by joining the Register

    D   encourage your friends to carry a donor card

A6 According to the leaflet, if you want to become a donor you should

    A   let your family know and join the Organ Donor Register

    B   take good care of your health and fitness

    C   donate money to the NHS

    D   visit your local hospital to find out more

Source B Level 1

Checking a plug

All modern appliances in the UK use the familiar square pin 13 amp plug. These plugs are used for handheld appliances such as hairdryers and vacuum cleaners, and larger appliances like microwave ovens. The plug and cable can suffer damage, particularly where they connect to portable appliances. Checking a plug and its cable does not require detailed electrical knowledge and these tips should help. With the plug removed from the socket, check the cable from end to end and ask the following questions:

1. **Is the cable securely attached to the appliance and the plug?**
2. **Is the cable cut, nicked or damaged in any way?**

There should preferably be no joints in the cable, and certainly no repairs with insulating tape.

Checking the plug

- Remove the plug from the socket and check the plug is not physically damaged
- Look for signs of overheating, such as discolouration
- Check that the plug conforms to British Standard BS 1363 – it should be marked on the back of the plug
- Check that the cable sheath is firmly clamped in the plug and that no coloured wires are showing.

For plugs that did not come fitted to the appliance, check that the cable is connected correctly as follows:

- Remove the plug from the socket, and remove the cover
- **Brown** to live (L)
- **Blue** to neutral (N)
- **Green-and-yellow** to earth (E)
- Check that the cord clamp holds the cable securely and that both of the screws are tight
- Check that the screws holding the three conductors are tight
- Check that the fuse is the correct rating and conforms to BS 1362 – refer to the manufacturer's instructions. The fuse should clip securely into its holder. It should not be loose and there should be no signs of overheating
- Replace the cover securely.

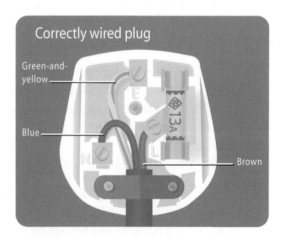

Correctly wired plug

Green-and-yellow

Blue

Brown

Most table lamps, standard lamps, televisions, videos, computers, mixers, blenders, power drills, jig saws, soldering irons will use 700W or less. Larger appliances such as washing machines, dishwashers, toasters, irons and heaters will use more than 700W. For the convenience of users, appliance equipment manufacturers have standardised on two plug fuse ratings (3A and 13A). For the appliances up to 700W, a 3A fuse is used. For those over 700W, a 13A fuse is used.

Questions 7 to 12 refer to Source B

B7   The *main* purpose of the leaflet is to

     A   instruct the reader how to check a plug
     B   show the reader what a plug looks like on the inside
     C   encourage people to become electricians
     D   advise the reader on how to install new electrical equipment

B8   There is a picture of the plug on page 17 of the leaflet to show

     A   the things that can go wrong with a plug
     B   what to do in an emergency
     C   that only a 13A fuse should be used
     D   how the inside of a plug should look when it is correctly wired

B9   If a plug is safe it should

     A   have a white plastic casing
     B   conform to British Standard BS 1363
     C   be fitted to an appliance
     D   always have a 3A fuse

B10   Which of the following statements is true?

     A   There are two main cables in a plug.
     B   The blue cable is connected to neutral.
     C   The brown cable is connected to earth.
     D   The square pin 13 amp plug is no longer in use.

B11   If you want to check a plug the first thing you should do is

     A   firmly replace the cover
     B   make sure the fuse is the correct rating
     C   remove the plug from the socket
     D   check the cable from end to end

B12   To check a fuse you should

     A   first reinforce the cable with insulating tape
     B   clip it into its holder
     C   make sure it is the correct rating and conforms to BS 1362
     D   make sure it is not tightly fitted

END OF QUESTIONS

Practice Reading assessment 2 Level 1

Practise another Level 1 Reading assessment by completing the following paper. Read Source A below carefully, then answer the 6 questions that follow. Next read Source B and answer the following 6 questions. There is only one correct answer to each question. You have 45 minutes to complete all 12 questions. You may use a dictionary if you wish.

Source A Level 1

Accom. Name	CYPROTEL POSEIDONIA			
No. of nights	7	10	11	14
Dept dates	Adult	Adult	Adult	Adult
01 Apr – 08 Apr	649	769	805	865
09 Apr – 21 Apr	539	659	699	815
22 Apr – 30 Apr	535	655	699	829
01 May – 16 May	575	705	749	885
17 May – 23 May	575	705	749	915
24 May – 28 May	669	805	845	915
29 May – 08 Jun	579	715	759	875
09 Jun – 22 Jun	569	699	745	875
23 Jun – 29 Jun	589	719	765	895
30 Jun – 06 Jul	589	719	765	895
07 Jul – 12 Jul	595	725	769	899
13 Jul – 18 Jul	615	745	789	939
19 Jul – 02 Aug	655	785	829	979
03 Aug – 15 Aug	699	849	899	1049
16 Aug – 22 Aug	699	849	899	1045
23 Aug – 28 Aug	719	869	919	995
29 Aug – 13 Sep	665	815	869	995
14 Sep – 20 Sep	655	805	855	995
21 Sep – 27 Sep	639	789	839	995
28 Sep – 11 Oct	615	745	789	919
12 Oct – 18 Oct	575	705	749	915
19 Oct – 23 Oct	645	779	819	885
24 Oct – 31 Oct	585	719	769	899

Package holiday prices shown are in pounds sterling and are the lowest per person for each date band, inclusive of transfers, taxes and duties

Cyprotel Poseidonia Beach Hotel

Surrounded by landscaped gardens, the Cyprotel Poseidonia Beach Hotel is situated on the beach between Limassol Bay and the bustling tourist area. There is a wide selection of bars, tavernas and shops all within walking distance and the Old Town is a convenient bus ride away. All bathrooms at the hotel were renovated during the winter months of 2005/2006.

Amenities: 24 hr reception
• Souvenir shop • Coffee shop
• Lobby and lounge bar
• Beach bar (May – Oct)
• Complimentary lounge chairs and sun umbrellas • Hairdressing salon
• Laundry service • Internet access (payable locally).

Leisure Activities: Outdoor swimming pool (covered and heated in winter)
• Tennis courts • Table Tennis
• Health Club • Jacuzzi • Sauna • Gym
• Mini golf & billiards – payable locally.

Entertainment: Animation team
• Theme nights.

For Children: Children's pool
• Playground with slide and climbing frame • Baby sitting on request
• Child highchairs • Early Meals/ Children's menu.

Accommodation: *Twin bedded rooms* (sleep 2/3 persons) at the Cyprotel Poseidonia are all spacious and well furnished. Rooms are equipped with air-conditioning, direct-dial telephone, hair dryer, fridges available (payable locally), radio with piped music, satellite TV, shower/bath and WC and a private balcony with sea or inland views. *Family rooms* sleep 2/4 and have either a sea or inland view. *Single rooms* with inland or sea views are also available.

Late checkout available – please speak to one of our Reservation Consultants for details

> ***Our Opinion:*** Suitable for all ages, the Cyprotel Poseidonia is a well maintained hotel that offers spacious rooms in a good location.

Price based on: All inclusive.
Units: 138 **Floors:** 7 **Lifts:** 2
Map ref.: H4 **Accom. Code:** 21218
Official Rating: 4 star

© Olympic Holidays

Each of **Questions A1** to **B12** is followed by four responses A, B, C and D. For each question select the best response. Write the question number and your choice of letter beside it.

Questions 1 to 6 refer to Source A

A1   The main purpose of this text is to

     A   advertise Cyprus as a holiday destination
     B   give information about the Cyprotel Poseidonia Beach Hotel
     C   explain how to book a holiday
     D   attract single people

A2   Information about the cost of the holiday is given

     A   at the travel agent
     B   under the heading 'Amenities'
     C   at the hotel reception
     D   in the table on the left

A3   The picture shows you

     A   how to windsurf
     B   how close the hotel is to the beach
     C   that the weather is always good
     D   that the hotel is not suitable for families

A4   The lowest price for an adult for 7 nights in June is

     A   £569
     B   £745
     C   £589
     D   £595

A5   The Cyprotel Poseidonia Beach Hotel is suitable for

     A   adults only
     B   water enthusiasts only
     C   families only
     D   people of all ages

A6   If you want to check out late you should

     A   speak to the hotel manager
     B   ring reception on the day of departure
     C   speak to a Reservation Consultant
     D   write to the hotel before your holiday

A Family Day Out to Remember

Travel between Embsay Station built in 1888 and the award winning station at Bolton Abbey. Your journey takes you through picturesque Yorkshire Dales scenery. Bolton Abbey Station is the ideal starting point for a pleasant one and a half mile walk to the ruins of the 12th century Priory. Venture a little further to picnic on the banks of the River Wharfe, or in the shade of Strid Wood where you will find the Cavendish Pavilion for refreshments.

1940s Weekend

Bolton Abbey Priory

© The Chatsworth Settlement Trustees, Bolton Abbey

Station facilities

Refreshments are available in the tearooms at Bolton Abbey and Embsay Stations. Both feature gift shops, including the famous bookshop at Embsay Station. There are picnic areas at all stations, including Holywell Halt, with facilities for the disabled at Bolton Abbey Station. Ample free parking is available at Embsay and Bolton Abbey Stations. There is even a coin operated children's self drive tram engine at Bolton Abbey Station.

Text © Embsay Station

Questions 7 to 12 refer to Source B

B7   Which of the following can you find at Holywell Halt?

    A   free parking
    B   disabled facilities
    C   a bookshop
    D   a picnic area

B8   In order to visit the 12th century Priory, you should take the train to

    A   Bolton Abbey Station
    B   Embsay Station
    C   Holywell Halt
    D   Cavendish Pavilion

B9   The pictures show

    A   what it was like in the 1940s
    B   scenes at and near the railway
    C   how to get to Bolton Abbey Priory
    D   what the trains look like

B10   The leaflet gives you information which would help you to

    A   apply for a job on the railway
    B   decide on a day out on the railway
    C   plan what to eat on your picnic
    D   work out how much the day out would cost

B11   This extract from the leaflet does not contain

    A   italic print
    B   pictures
    C   information
    D   bold print

B12   You can find facilities for the disabled at

    A   Bolton Abbey Station
    B   Embsay Station
    C   Holywell Halt
    D   Cavendish Pavilion

END OF QUESTIONS

Practice Reading assessment 3 Level 1 and Level 2

Practise a Level 1 and Level 2 Reading assessment by completing the following paper. Read each source carefully, then answer the questions that follow. There is only one correct answer to each question. You have 60 minutes to complete all 36 questions. You may use a dictionary if you wish.

Source A Level 1

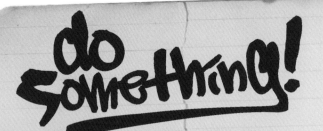

ZION ARTS CENTRE

February Half Term at Zion Arts Centre
Ages shown are guidelines only

£1 each day or £4 whole week

Masterclasses

For Further Education students

ODD Theatre Company
Community Theatre Masterclass for Performing Arts students
Tue 1–4pm

the young ones

Under 11 years

daily Sessions

Working towards Friday Finale

Samba
Straight from Rio, Republic of Swing teach you infectious samba funk rhythms
11–18 yrs Wed–Fri 1–2.30pm

Afro-Brazilian dance
Learn tribal rhythms and dance routines from Corpo Danca to perform with Republic of Swing
Wed–Fri 1–2.30pm

MC Class
Show No Mercy.... Spit with Hypes and Versie!
11–18yrs Mon–Fri 2.30–4.30pm

in between Sessions
Play computer games on Zion's giant projection screen in the theatre, watch films, chat with your friends, write down ideas for next half term and help shape the new www.zionarts.com

African Art + Culture Masterclass
Inspirational history seminar joining the dots between Hip Hop and the origins of Carnival
Thur 2–5pm

Action for Sustainable Living
How to work creatively with recycled materials for Arts students
Wed 2–4pm

Visual Arts
Fun and creative arts and craft activities
Mon–Fri 10–11.30am

DJ Workshop
Learn the tricks of the turntable with DJ Drizz
Mon–Fri 4.30–6.30pm

Streetdance
Bust some moves for Friday's Finale
8–15 yrs
Mon–Fri 10–12pm

The Dark
Sonic Art Installation experience with drama workshops about 18th century slave trade
Mon–Fri 10am–12pm

Supported by
The National Lottery
through the Heritage Lottery Fund
Heritage Lottery Fund

Zion Youth Forum
Zion Arts Centre is looking to set up a youth forum for you to lead the way and have a say!
Ask to chat with a member of Zion's creative staff at any time during the week for more information or phone 0161 226 1912 to get involved!

Kite Making
Build your very own flying machine!
For 7–11 years
Friday 2–3.30pm

Radio
Taster sessions ahead of Zion's very own Youth Internet Radio Station TBC

Big Movie Screening
A different alternative film each day
Mon–Fri 2–4pm

Friday Finale
Come together in Zion's theatre to share and showcase your week's work + DJ set from Drizz
FREE (recommended £2 entry donation) 7pm

Zion Arts Afterschool Club
Coming soon to a Primary School near YOU! If you attend a primary school in Hulme, we will be running afterschool creative sessions in art, dance, drama and music up until your summer holidays.
Keep a look out for info from your teachers soon... and sign up!

Places are limited. Book now! see overleaf...

MANCHESTER CITY COUNCIL

Neighbourhood Renewal Unit

© Zion Arts Centre

Each of **Questions A1** to **F36** is followed by four responses **A**, **B**, **C** and **D**. For each question select the best response. Write the question number and your choice of letter beside it.

Questions 1 to 6 refer to Source A

A1   The *main* purpose of this text is to

    A   encourage readers to work during the holidays
    B   improve readers' dance skills
    C   inform readers about sessions at the Zion Arts Centre
    D   advise readers on how to spend their money

A2   Which of the following statements is true?

    A   There is an age limit for entry to the Big Movie Screening.
    B   The centre is supported by The National Lottery.
    C   The Arts Centre already has a youth forum.
    D   There are no sessions on Monday.

A3   To get involved in the Zion Youth Forum you should

    A   pay £4
    B   showcase your week's work
    C   attend the Afterschool Club
    D   phone 0161 226 1912

A4   The writer informs you that

    A   children under 11 are not allowed to go to the centre
    B   places in the sessions are limited
    C   courses on Saturday and Sunday will cost extra
    D   Further Education students are not welcome

A5   According to the times given in the leaflet, you could

    A   go to all the sessions for Samba **and** Afro-Brazilian dance
    B   go to the African Art + Culture Masterclass on Wednesday
    C   go to all the sessions for Samba **and** the DJ Workshop
    D   go to the sessions in March

A6   After you have read this, an appropriate action would be to

    A   book a place on one or more of the sessions
    B   get a job during your holidays
    C   learn how to make kites
    D   raise money for the Zion Arts Centre

Source B Level 1

File Edit File Edit View Favorites Tools Help

⬅ Back ▾ ➡ ▪ ▪ ▪ 🔍 Search

Address [   ] ▾ ➡ Go Links »

🔲 Pop-up blocked. To see this pop-up or additional options click here...   ✕

Motoring

Practical test for cars explained

Your driving test will start with an eyesight check and some vehicle safety questions. The driving part of your test will last about 40 minutes. Your examiner will be looking for an overall safe standard of driving.

The practical driving test (car)

Practical tests are generally available at all permanent test centres. Saturday and weekday evening tests, subject to resources being available, are offered at a premium rate. The driving test is straightforward and has been designed to see if you:
- can drive safely
- know The Highway Code and can demonstrate this through your driving.

What will the test include?

The test will include an eyesight check which requires you to read a number plate that is a certain distance away. For more information about the eyesight check please use the 'Driving eyesight requirements' link below. If you fail this, your test will be stopped. You will then be asked two vehicle safety check questions and be examined on your general driving and two reversing exercises chosen from:
- reversing around a corner
- turning in the road
- reverse parking

You may also be asked to carry out an emergency stop exercise.

(Driving eyesight requirements)

What happens during the test?

During the driving test the examiner will give you directions which you should follow. Test routes will include a range of typical road and traffic conditions.

Throughout the test you should drive in the way your instructor has taught you. If you make a mistake, don't worry too much; it might be a less serious driving fault and may not affect your result. The examiner will be looking for an overall safe standard.

You can make up to 15 driving faults and still pass the test. However, if you commit one serious or dangerous fault you will fail the test.

After the practical test

When the driving test is over, the examiner will tell you whether you passed or failed. You can request feedback on your test from the examiner, who will then go through your performance during the test.

🌐 Internet

Questions 7 to 12 refer to Source B

B7 The main purpose of the web page is to

    A   sell you a car
    B   encourage you to have your eyesight tested
    C   tell you about the driving test
    D   persuade you to learn to drive

B8 The reversing exercise could include

    A   an emergency stop
    B   driving forwards into a parking space
    C   answering a vehicle safety check question
    D   making a turn in the road

B9 Which of the following statements is true?

    A   You can make 16 driving faults and still pass your test.
    B   You are allowed to make one serious fault.
    C   Instructors don't record less serious faults.
    D   You will fail your test if you make one serious fault.

B10 Which one of the following is not contained in the layout of the web page?

    A   italics for emphasis
    B   sub-headings to organise the information
    C   information to help the reader
    D   bullet points to clarify information

B11 If you want to pay less for your test you should

    A   book it for a Saturday
    B   book it for a weekday
    C   book it for a weekday evening
    D   book it in advance

B12 To find out more about the eyesight test you should

    A   go to see your optician
    B   make sure you can see all number plates
    C   use the link given on the web page
    D   wear glasses when driving

Source C Level 2

London Calling

Imagine a map of the 600 square miles of teeming Metropolis that is London. Now point to the centre.

Chances are, your finger is pointing somewhere close to the new £4.3million, YHA London Central, which has just unveiled 294 new beds for young people and international travellers.

Less than a mile away, is the stunning new St Pancras International. It's bang opposite YHA London St Pancras, which is undergoing a £1million face-lift ready for the 2008 season and will offer improved accommodation for families, mature travellers and groups.

There has never been a better time to stay with YHA in London; in fact there has never been a better time to be in London, full stop. As Europe's largest City and home to more than 8 million

people, London is buzzing as preparations gather momentum for the forthcoming 2012 Olympics. Brand new venues such as the new O2 arena (formerly The Dome) are springing up, and this will host 150 world-class new music and sporting events this year alone.

But with more historic landmarks per square mile than just about anywhere else on the planet, you don't have to be a sport or music fan to enjoy this 2,000-year-old city. The great news is that many of London's best museums, galleries and historic attractions are free – so your trip to the capital needn't cost the earth. From YHA London Central, you can almost hear Big Ben's iconic

13-ton bell ringing, telling you to get up and get busy, as there's so much to see and so little time. With Oxford Street, the newly revamped Telecom Tower and cosmopolitan Soho on the doorstep, guests can walk right into the heart of the city, as they step out of the front door. Over at St Pancras, YHA early birds can Channel-hop on the new high-speed train link and be in Paris before breakfast.

These are just two of YHA's safe, modern bases from which visitors can explore and enjoy London. They are already popular, so book early!

Book now!
Visit www.yha.org.uk or call 01629 592 700 for details.

Questions 13 to 17 refer to Source C

C13   The main purpose of this text is to

   A   persuade the reader to go to the 2012 Olympics
   B   show the reader what can be done in London
   C   explain how to find the Youth Hostels
   D   persuade the reader to stay with the YHA in London

C14   The text informs you that

   A   the place once known as The Dome is now called the O2 Arena
   B   the sound of Big Ben can be heard across the whole of London
   C   single people cannot stay at YHA London St Pancras
   D   a trip to London will not cost a lot

C15   The pictures are used effectively to show

   A   what the youth hostels are like
   B   some of the places to visit in London
   C   how easy it is to get round London on a bike
   D   that London is a large city

C16   The writer implies that London is

   A   a cheap place to visit
   B   a boring place to visit
   C   a dangerous place to visit
   D   an exciting place to visit

C17   Which of the following actions does the writer of the text hope people will take after reading it?

   A   Visit the O2 Arena.
   B   Catch the high speed train link to Paris.
   C   Book a place to stay with the YHA in London.
   D   Listen to Big Ben's 13-ton bell ringing.

Source D Level 2

Membership Department
PO Box 39, Warrington
WA5 7WD
Telephone 0844 800 1895
minicom 0844 800 4410
www.nationaltrust.org.uk

2008

Dear Member,

Thank you for your continued support as we enter 2008. All of us at the National Trust hope that you are intending to spend many delightful days out visiting our houses and gardens and experiencing the unique atmosphere, history and beauty behind some of the Nation's most celebrated places.

Ask your friends to join us

It's going to be an exciting and busy year for the National Trust, with seasonal events, fairs, markets and special anniversaries happening across the country, providing you with plenty of opportunities to do something out of the ordinary. And what could be better than sharing unforgettable moments with the people you love. So why not introduce a friend to National Trust membership so that you can make the most of doing things together. Even the simple things in life, like a lazy afternoon walk amongst ancient trees; tucking into just-baked cake in a traditional tea-room, or picking up some home-grown fruit and veg at a local farmer's market are so much better shared.

A shared history

By passing on the benefits of National Trust membership to a like-minded friend, you are passing on so much more than just free entry to hundreds of historic houses and gardens. There is the protection and conservation of buildings, paintings, textiles, treasures, traditional skills, hectares of countryside, wild habitats and miles of coastline in our care. And there is the deep satisfaction that comes from knowing that every penny of every membership makes a real and tangible difference to it all.

It's your National Trust, pass it on

Nothing could be easier or more rewarding. Simply pass the form, on the back of this letter, to your friend or ask them to call our Membership Department on 0844 800 1895. If they join before 31 March 2008, they can get a year's membership at 2007 prices, and if they pay by Direct Debit they will also receive three months' absolutely free. What's more, once they have joined we will send you an exclusive National Trust branded umbrella as a thank you for the extra support.

Wishing you a happy and healthy year ahead.

Yours sincerely,

A Silvester

Anne Silvester
Head of Customer Care

Questions 18 to 22 refer to Source D

D18 The main purpose of this text is to

    A   extend the membership of the National Trust
    B   wish the reader a Happy New Year
    C   inform the reader about the achievements of the National Trust
    D   publicise the National Trust through the sale of umbrellas

D19 The tone of the text can best be described as

    A   angry
    B   indifferent
    C   encouraging
    D   relaxed

D20 Which one of the following actions do the writers of the text hope the reader might take?

    A   Pin the letter on their noticeboard at work.
    B   Celebrate a special anniversary in the countryside.
    C   Campaign for the protection of the environment.
    D   Encourage a friend to join the National Trust.

D21 The text informs you that

    A   the National Trust does not hold fundraising events
    B   membership of the National Trust is free for a year
    C   the money gained from membership makes a real difference
    D   2007 was the National Trust's most successful year

D22 The emphasis of the three sub-headings is on

    A   visiting different places
    B   friendship and sharing
    C   history
    D   the cost of joining the National Trust

The following two questions refer to sources C and D

D23 One similarity between texts C and D is that

    A   they both address the reader directly
    B   neither text gives contact details
    C   they both tell you how much it will cost to join the organisation
    D   they both focus on things to do in London

D24 Which of the following statements is correct?

    A   Both texts use images for effect.
    B   Both texts give information about how to join the organisation.
    C   Both texts are organised by sub-headings.
    D   Both texts are informative and persuasive.

HOW LONG ARE YOU HERE FOR?

Driving under the influence of drink and drugs remains a serious problem. In Manchester City alone, there have been 115 collisions in the past three years in which the contributory factor has been either alcohol or drugs. This resulted in the death or serious injury of 142 people, equating to approximately one serious or fatal collision every ten days caused by a driver under the influence.

Despite recent progress made in highlighting the dangers of drinking and driving, the problem still persists, and the trend appears to be on the increase with young drivers aged 17–24. There is also evidence that drug-driving is on the increase. In the last twenty years there has been a six-fold increase in the number of people killed in road accidents who had traces of illegal drugs in their body.

We are asking drivers to consider alternative means of transport, particularly over the Christmas period when a higher proportion of people on the streets of Manchester are likely to be under the influence.

And pedestrians too – be aware of the risks associated with walking around the city under the influence during the festive season. Most drivers will not slow down or stop if you decide to step off the pavement!

The best way to get around is by bus, train, tram and taxi.
You'll avoid the frustration of traffic jams and hours spent trying to find a parking space. You'll also be able to get into the swing of the party, and on Fridays and Saturdays there are special Nightbus services to get you home right into the small hours.

For further information about public transport services in Greater Manchester ring 0870 608 2608 or visit www.gmpte.com

Questions 25 to 29 refer to Source E

E25 The text argues that

    A   people should not drink alcohol or take drugs
    B   public transport is the cheapest way to travel
    C   drivers should consider using public transport over Christmas
    D   the legal age for driving should be raised to 25

E26 The text informs the reader that

    A   more people are driving while under the influence of drugs
    B   there have been 85 collisions in Manchester City in the previous 3 years
    C   drivers never slow down or stop for pedestrians
    D   there are special Nightbus services during the week

E27 The pictures of tombstones are effective because they

    A   show you that you will die unless you use public transport
    B   emphasise how many deaths have been caused by drink- or drug-driving
    C   show the same thing several times
    D   make you think about graveyards

E28 The tone of the writing could best be described as

    A   jolly
    B   angry
    C   sarcastic
    D   serious

E29 What action does the writer hope drivers will take over the Christmas period, after reading the text?

    A   Avoid the crowded city centre.
    B   Stop going to parties on Fridays and Saturdays.
    C   Always travel with someone over the age of 24.
    D   Make more use of buses, trains, trams and taxis.

Source F Level 2

WORK & STUDY

What are Apprenticeships?

You do on-the-job training and study for an NVQ. Usually they take between one and four years. There are Apprenticeships available in more than 80 industries (from accounting to transport) and you get paid. It also gives you the opportunity to go on to HE.

What it feels like to be an Apprentice...

David, 21, from Cornwall tells you...

"I was a bit naughty at school but loved practical lessons like design and technology and helping my dad fix the car. At 16 I became an Apprentice helicopter engineer! I got paid – so had a bit of cash in my pocket – and did an NVQ in engineering. I'm usually stripping engines, but last year I was filmed hanging out of a helicopter for a TV show. Amazing! I want to be a pilot now and I'm looking into degrees. This has taught me I can do anything I want."

GO PLACES – FAST

What you can study at HIGHER EDUCATION: Three ways to do it

HE qualification: Honours degree (either Bachelor of Arts (BA) or Bachelor of Science (BSc). This is the most common qualification.

What that entails: A 3–4 year full-time course studying at uni or college. Can also be taken part-time. The sandwich course includes a year at work.

Example of courses: Drama and screen studies, adventure tourism, chemistry, art history.

Pros: Gives you the chance to study a subject in-depth. Wide choice of professional job options. Can go on to gain other professional qualifications e.g. a Master's degree or PhD.

HE qualification: Foundation Degree

What that entails: two years if studied full-time (part-time is often 3–4 years) where you work with an employer and study.

Example of courses: tourism, aircraft engineering, new media design, veterinary nursing, automotive manufacturing. There are about 1,300 different options.

Pros: Get stuck into a job (and see if you like it!). Often employers offer you a job at the end of your study. It gives you the option to progress on to further HE qualifications and to the final year of specified degrees.

HE qualification: Higher National Diploma/Certificate (HND/HNC) or Diploma of Higher Education

What that entails: HNCs take a year full-time or two years part-time. Full-time HNDs or Dip of HE take two years, and can also be taken part-time. While you're studying you do work-placements (and get paid for them!).

Example of courses: vocational subjects such as photography, beauty and holistics, public administration and theatre design.

Pros: You learn something with a job in mind. You can convert to a degree with an extra year of study.

Questions 30 to 34 refer to Source F

F30   The main purpose of this text is to

     A   advertise apprenticeships for helicopter engineers
     B   give alternatives to full-time or part-time education
     C   raise awareness of Higher Education qualifications and courses
     D   inform the reader about the world of work

F31   The text informs you that

     A   an honours degree can be taken full-time or part-time
     B   apprenticeships usually take between four and six years
     C   HNCs cannot be taken as part-time courses
     D   a Master's degree is taken before an Honours degree

F32   The pictures are effective because they show

     A   that you earn a lot of money as an apprentice
     B   the helicopter that David pilots
     C   that you can dress casually as an apprentice
     D   that David is happy in what he has chosen to do

F33   David's words suggest he

     A   is pleased that he did an apprenticeship
     B   regrets doing an apprenticeship
     C   wishes he had done something different
     D   always disliked school

F34   According to the text, which of the following actions would be most appropriate for someone who wanted to pursue a career in photography?

     A   Leave school at sixteen and practise taking photographs.
     B   Study for a Bachelor of Science (BSc) Honours degree.
     C   Study for an HND, HNC or Dip of HE.
     D   Travel the world before deciding what to do.

The following two questions refer to sources E and F

F35   Texts E and F both

     A   give contact numbers for further information
     B   tell you the advantages of taking the advised course of action
     C   criticise the behaviour of young people
     D   focus on things to do in Manchester

F36   Which of the following statements is correct?

     A   Both texts are only relevant to people under 25.
     B   Both texts use the same font throughout.
     C   Both texts are organised by sub-headings.
     D   Both texts are designed to have a visual impact.

END OF QUESTIONS

Practice Reading assessment 4 Level 1 and Level 2

Practise another Level 1 and Level 2 Reading assessment by completing the following paper. Read each source carefully, then answer the questions that follow. There is only one correct answer to each question. You have 60 minutes to complete all 36 questions. You may use a dictionary if you wish.

Source A Level 1

Go further with a 16-18 Metro Student Card

If you're a full-time student aged 16-18 years old then this is the Metro card for you. And you can do more than just go to school or college with this pass. Why not use it to visit friends, go to the cinema, or bowling - the list is endless!

To get a 16-18 Metro Student Card you need to be:
- Aged under 19 years on 1 September 07
- In full-time further education

Price

The 16-18 Metro Student Card is valid on the whole Metro system - look at the Metro map to see where you can go.

1 week	4 weeks
£8.00	£29.50

How to buy one

You will need to complete the application form overleaf and take to any Nexus TravelShop, along with proof of your age and some student identification (with academic dates shown).

You will also need a passport sized photograph, which is also available from the TravelShops.

How to renew

Once you have your 16-18 Metro Student photocard you have the option of renewing at:
- Any Nexus TravelShop
- Calling the renewal hotline on **0191 203 3315** (open Monday to Friday, 9.00am to 4.00pm)
- Renew online at **www.nexus.org.uk**

Nexus TravelShops

You can find Nexus TravelShops at:
Central Station Metro, Gateshead Interchange, Haymarket Metro station, Heworth Interchange, Four Lane Ends Interchange, MetroCentre, Monument Metro station, North Shields Metro station, Park Lane Interchange, South Shields, Fowler Street.

Large print and alternative formats available on request: tel 0191 203 3333 or email metro.marketing@nexus.org.uk

16-18 Metro Student Card application form

Please complete in block capitals

Title: Mr / Miss   First name:

Surname:

Address:

Postcode:

Email address:

Mobile no:

Nearest Metro station:

School/College:

Pass required   (please tick):

1 week ☐   4 weeks ☐

Payment   (please tick):

Cash ☐   Switch, Solo, Delta ☐

Credit Card ☐

Data Protection Act: Please tick here if you want to receive further information on Metro, special offers or discounts ☐

For office use only

TravelShop:

Photocard no: MS

Date:

Terms & conditions   CONDITIONS OF USE

1. All 16-18 tickets and accompanying photocard remain the property of Nexus
2. 16-18 tickets are only valid when presented with a valid photocard bearing the same number. They must be shown together whenever requested.
3. 16-18 tickets are not transferable. They may only be used by the person identified on the accompanying photocard.
4. 16-18 tickets can only be used within the zones validated on the ticket.
5. A 1 week 16-18 ticket is valid for 7 days; a 4 week 16-18 ticket is valid for 28 days. A Metro Student Card shall not be valid for use outside the period shown on the ticket.
6. No person shall (i) alter, deface, mutilate or destroy a 16-18 ticket (ii) use or attempt to use a 16-18 ticket which shall have been in any respect materially altered, defaced or mutilated.
7. Use of a 16-18 ticket shall be governed by the Tyne and Wear Passenger Transport Act 1979, the Bylaws which relate to Metro and Bus Premises and the conditions of Carriage and Passenger Regulations applying to the Tyne and Wear Metro.

© Nexus

Each of **Questions A1** to **F36** is followed by four responses A, B, C and D. For each question select the best response. Write the question number and your choice of letter beside it.

Questions 1 to 6 refer to Source A

A1   The main purpose of this text is to

    A   show the reader the Metro rail routes

    B   tell the reader when a rail pass is required

    C   persuade the reader to buy a Metro Student Card

    D   tell the reader about Nexus TravelShops

A2   To get a Metro Student Card you must be

    A   living in the area

    B   in part-time education

    C   aged 16–21

    D   aged 16–18 and in full-time further education

A3   The application form

    A   requires a parent's or guardian's signature

    B   should be completed in block capitals

    C   requires the applicant's date of birth

    D   should be completed in blue or black pen

A4   If you decide to buy a Metro Student Card, you will need

    A   access to online services

    B   a bank account

    C   to go to a Nexus TravelShop

    D   to be 19 on 1 September 07

A5   When applying for a Metro Student Card you do **not** need

    A   a passport sized photograph

    B   a map of the Metro

    C   proof of your age

    D   student identification

A6   To renew a Metro Student Photocard on a Saturday you could

    A   renew online at www.nexus.org.uk

    B   call the renewal hotline on 0191 203 3315

    C   visit the Nexus TravelShop at the airport

    D   ask a parent or guardian to do it for you

Source B Level 1

Back ▾   Search

Address   Go   Links »

Pop-up blocked. To see this pop-up or additional options click here...   ✕

animaljobsdirect.com

Zoo Keeper

Zoo keepers are responsible for the day-to-day care and welfare of animals in a zoo, wildlife/safari park or special collection. Animals must be kept in the correct environment to keep them physically and psychologically healthy. Keepers carry out such tasks as 'mucking out', cleaning and filling water troughs, replenishing bedding and monitoring temperatures. They order food and bedding and ensure animals are fed according to their individual needs. Another important aspect of the work is observing the animals for any signs of injury or illness and keeping detailed healthcare records, normally on a computer.

A zoo keeper's typical working week is 37.5 to 40 hours. Overtime may be available. Animals must be cared for every day of the year, so zoo keepers work on a rota to cover all periods.

Zoo keepers may work outside or indoors, depending on the animals they care for. Keepers wear a uniform, normally an overall that is supplied by their employer. They may work alone, or in pairs or groups for some tasks. The work is unsuitable for people with allergies to fur or hair.

The starting salary could be the national minimum wage. Experienced zoo keepers might earn £15,000. The highest salary might be around £21,500.

Zoo keepers need to: be enthusiastic about animals, be interested in animal biology, be patient with both the public and animals, and have a pleasant, friendly manner and good spoken communication skills. They need to be observant, reliable and punctual, physically fit, safety-conscious, and have basic computer skills and a driving licence for safari parks.

Keepers work at zoos, safari/wildlife parks, bird collections and aquariums. There are probably only about 1,500 people employed in this work. Entry is very competitive, and there are many more applicants than vacancies. It may be possible to start as a trainee at 16 but some employers set a minimum age of 18. Some people may be able to train on an Apprenticeship.

Apprenticeships which may be available in England are Young Apprenticeships, pre-Apprenticeships, Apprenticeships and Advanced Apprenticeships. To find out which one is most appropriate log onto www.apprenticeships.org.uk

Internet

Questions 7 to 12 refer to Source B

B7   The main purpose of this text is to

   A   persuade you to work with animals
   B   give you information about zoo-keeping as a career
   C   argue that zoo keepers should be paid more
   D   advertise vacancies in zoo-keeping

B8   How many people are employed in this work?

   A   4,000
   B   21,000
   C   1,500
   D   Over 40,000

B9   Why might a zoo keeper need computer skills?

   A   To keep records on people visiting the zoo
   B   To gain a higher salary
   C   To record the hours they have worked
   D   To keep records on animals' healthcare

B10   Which of the following is not a requirement for zoo keepers?

   A   An interest in animal biology
   B   The ability to swim
   C   Physical fitness
   D   An awareness of possible dangers

B11   You would not be suitable for the job if you

   A   have an allergy to fur or hair
   B   are punctual and reliable
   C   are physically fit
   D   are prepared to do overtime

B12   To get more information about apprenticeships you need to

   A   visit your nearest zoo
   B   visit www.animaljobsdirect.com
   C   visit www.apprenticeships.org.uk
   D   work part-time in a zoo

WELCOME AND OVERVIEW

What are Discovery Visits?

English Heritage now offers Discovery Visits for schools – an exciting range of site-based workshops and interactive tours that take a fresh look at history and reveal the cross-curricular potential of our sites. Enjoy sessions led by specialist educators and site staff which bring our buildings and landscapes to life.

"Feeling the heavy chain mail, you wonder if you're really safe..."

Covering the breadth of English history, our varied programme of memorable encounters is tailored to meet the learning needs of groups across all Key Stages. Some sessions also link to other subjects including literacy, science, drama, PSHE, citizenship, art or music.

Choose from:

WORKSHOPS
involving different teaching and learning approaches including storytelling, construction, problem-solving, role-play, games, handling objects and much more. Pupils can meet characters from the past, make a medieval tile or crack secret codes used during World War II.

INTERACTIVE TOURS
offering rich, fun and interactive learning experiences that are led by site staff who know their sites inside out! Pupils can get involved in observation, questioning, discussion, artefact-handling or role-play to discover the hidden histories of our properties.

"Thank you for an inspiring time – the pupils will talk about it for ages!"

This brochure lists the properties where you can experience Discovery Visits in addition to your usual Free Educational Visit. For details of all English Heritage sites you can visit with your group, see the **Visits Guide** to free educational visits sent to your school, or see **www.english-heritage.org.uk**

COST
At just £60 per school group for a Discovery Visit (unless otherwise stated), these are excellent value for a school trip full of surprises.

© English Heritage Education 2007

Questions 13 to 17 refer to Source C

C13   This English Heritage leaflet is aiming to

    A   recruit new members
    B   persuade schools to hold lessons outdoors
    C   inform schools about Discovery Visits
    D   raise funds

C14   As well as looking at history, Discovery Visit sessions also link to

    A   literacy only
    B   a range of other subjects
    C   no other school subjects
    D   every school subject

C15   The purpose of the picture is to show you

    A   the number of schools which visit the sites
    B   that children enjoy these visits
    C   an English Heritage site
    D   that the activities are in classrooms

C16   Discovery Visits are intended for

    A   Key Stage 1 pupils
    B   Key Stage 2 pupils
    C   Key Stage 3 pupils
    D   pupils across the Key Stages

C17   After teachers have read this, the writers hope they will

    A   want to teach history
    B   apply for a job as a specialist educator
    C   arrange a Discovery Visit
    D   book a Free Educational Visit

Source D Level 2

a cleaner, greener place to be

A brighter future for waste management in Greater Manchester

by tackling the myths

Your questions answered

When we talk about recycling and waste handling facilities, people can get the wrong impression. The reality is that the modern facilities we are planning to build across Greater Manchester will be bright and clean, and virtually all planned improvements will take place at existing sites. So, let's answer some of the common questions that you may have:

Q: Will the facilities smell?
A: They will be almost odour free.
- Materials will be removed from all facilities on a regular basis.
- The new technologies operate in contained environments to keep odours within buildings.
- Air within the buildings will be treated to remove odours.

Q: Will they cause a lot of noise?
A: Facilities are designed to keep noise levels to an absolute minimum.
- Buildings are constructed with noise-reduction cladding.
- Machinery is used in enclosed areas and is inspected regularly to minimise operational noise.

Q: Will they produce litter?
A: The facilities are designed to minimise dust and litter.
- Materials will be securely contained whilst on site and during removal.
- Facilities will be kept clean by manual and mechanical sweeping.

Q: Will we be building new incinerators in Greater Manchester?
A: No, but our existing incinerator in Bolton will continue to be used.

Q: How will they deal with traffic?
A: All facilities are designed for better traffic management.
- The largest sites are already served by rail links.
- Vehicle movements are usually kept separate from private cars, making the sites safer for everyone.
- Onsite traffic management systems will be used on some sites to minimise queuing.

Q: What happens to the fuel that is created from MBT?
A: The 275,000 tonnes of waste derived fuel produced in the Greater Manchester facilities will be transported by rail to be used by a proposed private sector facility outside Greater Manchester – replacing fossil fuels and protecting jobs in that industrial area.

Q: Will any of the facilities be open to the public?
A: Yes. Significant improvements in our Household Waste Recycling Centres will make it easier for you to recycle a wide range of materials. Education centres will also be developed at major facilities, with dedicated staff to explain the new facilities and encourage parties of school children and adults to Reduce, Reuse and Recycle more.

GMWDA

Questions 18 to 22 refer to Source D

D18   The planned improvements will

    A   increase unemployment in the area
    B   not be open to the public
    C   nearly all be made at existing sites
    D   pump clean air into the buildings

D19   The incinerator is in

    A   Rochdale
    B   Greater Manchester
    C   Central Manchester
    D   Bolton

D20   Which of the following does the sheet **not** use?

    A   Bullet points
    B   Bold print
    C   Italics
    D   An illustration

D21   The facilities mentioned in the leaflet

    A   have been built in Greater Manchester
    B   are not built yet
    C   have an Education Centre
    D   are smelly and noisy

D22   Traffic issues will be dealt with by

    A   an efficient queuing system
    B   rail links to the big sites
    C   the introduction of traffic lights
    D   a traffic management inspector

The following two questions refer to sources C and D

D23   Both Sources C and D

    A   use a question and answer approach to convey information
    B   use a picture to make their leaflet look interesting
    C   give contact details so the reader can take further action
    D   use bullet points to organise information

D24   Both sources C and D

    A   inform the reader
    B   ask the reader to contribute money
    C   offer interactive tours
    D   deal with an environmental issue

Source E Level 2

Spring 2008

MAMMA MIA!
Prince of Wales Theatre

A mother. A daughter. 3 possible dads.
And a trip down the aisle you'll never forget!

MAMMA MIA! is the global phenomenon based
on the songs of ABBA. Timeless songs such as
Dancing Queen, *I Have a Dream* and *Voulez
Vous* are ingeniously woven into an enchanting
tale of love, laughter and friendship.

'The perfect ticket for a feel-good night out!'
Daily Telegraph

'Sensational… infectious theatrical entertainment'
Financial Times

Group rate: 10+: Two top prices reduced
to £39 (Mon – Fri eves + Fri mat)

40+: Top two prices reduced to £35
(Mon – Fri eves + Fri mat)

Produced by little star

Ralph   Tamsin
FIENNES GREIG
Janet   Ken
McTEER STOTT

GOD
of CARNAGE
a new play by
YASMINA REZA
translated by
CHRISTOPHER HAMPTON
directed by
MATTHEW WARCHUS

Produced by David Pugh and Dafydd Rogers

GOD OF CARNAGE
Gielgud Theatre

What happens when two sets of parents meet up
to deal with the unruly behaviour of their children.
A calm and rational debate between grownups
about the need to teach kids how to behave
properly? Or a hysterical night of name calling,
tantrums and tears before bedtime?

Boys will be boys, but the adults are usually
worse – much worse!

'A crackling night of electrifying comedy acting'
Daily Telegraph

*'All four actors excel in Matthew Warchus's deft
production which is full of delights'*
The Guardian

Group rate: 8+: Best available reduced
to £35 (Mon – Thurs + Wed mat

Tel: 0844 482 5100

groupsales@delmack.co.uk

Questions 25 to 29 refer to Source E

E25 The writer of *God of Carnage* is

A   Christopher Hampton
B   Benny Andersson
C   Yasmina Reza
D   Matthew Warchus

E26 *God of Carnage* features

A   one actor
B   two actors
C   three actors
D   four actors

E27 The two posters effectively

A   highlight the title of each play
B   show a photograph of each play
C   include extracts from reviews
D   give information about ticket prices

E28 The main purpose of this page is to

A   list all plays showing in London
B   give detailed play reviews
C   show pictures of the writers
D   advertise reductions for groups

E29 The producers of this page hope that, having read it, readers will

A   find out more about the plays
B   go to see the plays
C   write a review for one or both plays
D   wait for prices to be reduced

▲ New Metallic Graphite

◀ New Metallic Red

Brushed Stainless Steel ▶

The EXCLUSIVE Scotts of Stow Stainless Steel Thermal Cafetière. Now available in two sensational new 'metallic' finishes Only £19.95

For connoisseurs, there's nothing better than a freshly brewed cup of coffee made in the traditional French way using a proper cafetière or coffee press. It's a method of brewing which is said to extract maximum flavour from ground beans, retaining more of the aromatic coffee oils and allowing you to make coffee just as you like it, because you can choose how long it brews before you 'plunge'. The Scotts of Stow thermal cafetière is designed for maximum heat retention. The high quality stainless steel body has a twin-wall insulated construction that keeps the contents ready to drink for considerably longer than an ordinary cafetière. In fact, in the Scotts of Stow test kitchen, it maintained the contents at over 60°C for more than two hours. Featuring a thermal 'lock' to seal in warmth and aroma, a super-fine steel mesh that traps the grounds superbly, and a stay cool handle and knob for easy plunging and pouring. The 1¾ pint capacity makes 8 demi-tasse coffees or 4 generous breakfast cups. Overall height 10¾".

Two new finishes for 2008

Our famous cafetière now comes in two new finishes for 2008. As well as classic brushed Stainless Steel, it is also available in a stunning, subtly reflective Metallic Red or Metallic Graphite, both guaranteed to raise comments of admiration at the dining table.

Please specify colour when ordering Metallic finish.

119 1728 Stainless Steel Finish Cafetière £19.95
131 0925 Metallic Finish Cafetière £19.95

ORDER ANYTIME 0844-482-2020

© Scotts of Stow

Questions 30 to 34 refer to Source F

F30   The purpose of this text is to

  A   sell you a Thermal Cafetière from Scotts of Stow
  B   show you how to make really good French coffee
  C   buy one cafetière and then get the second one free
  D   inform the readers about different kinds of coffee

F31   The Thermal Cafetière's body is made of

  A   metallic graphite
  B   aromatic oils
  C   steel mesh
  D   stainless steel

F32   The purpose of the photos is to

  A   show what the Thermal Cafetière looks like
  B   show the three finishes that the Thermal Cafetière comes in
  C   show the actual size of the cafetières
  D   show how to make good coffee in the cafètieres

F33   Which of the following does the article **not** claim?

  A   The Thermal Cafetière makes 4 large breakfast cups of coffee or
       8 demi-tasse coffees.
  B   The test kitchen showed the Thermal Cafetière kept its heat for over two hours.
  C   You can choose how long to brew the coffee before you press the plunger.
  D   These Thermal Cafetières are cheaper than all the others on the market.

F34   The information is effective because

  A   it compares different kinds of cafetière
  B   it uses bold and italic fonts and bullet points
  C   it gives useful detail about Thermal Cafetières
  D   the language is difficult to read

The following two questions refer to sources E and F

F35   Sources E and F are both

  A   adverts
  B   advice sheets
  C   information sheets
  D   news articles

F36   One similarity between both texts is that they both

  A   offer a personal point of view
  B   inform you about what they are selling
  C   use many illustrations
  D   use informal language

END OF QUESTIONS

Unit 2 Writing

To determine your level in Writing you will take a timed test. In this test, you will complete a writing task. If you take the Level 1 test it will last for 45 minutes and you will be asked to write to inform. The combined Level 1 and 2 test will last for one hour and you will write to inform and persuade. You will be allowed to use a dictionary in the exam.

The different levels

For Writing Level 1 you need to:

- write clearly with an appropriate level of detail
- present information in an order that makes sense
- write appropriately for purpose and audience
- use correct grammar
- make sure that your meaning is clear
- make sure your punctuation and spelling are accurate.

For Writing Level 2 you need to:

- present information/ideas concisely, logically and persuasively
- present information on complex subjects concisely and clearly
- use a range of different styles of writing for different purposes
- use a range of sentence structures, including complex sentences
- punctuate accurately using commas, apostrophes and inverted commas
- make sure your written work has accurate grammar, punctuation and spelling and that meaning is clear

Tackling writing tasks

In writing tasks follow these six steps to make the most of your time.

1	Read the task
2	Identify features of the task
3	Gather your ideas

4	Organise your ideas
5	Write
6	Check, correct and improve your writing

The exam paper

Look at page 47 – this shows you what the front page of a Writing paper will look like. Always make sure you understand exactly what is required of you. The annotations given on page 47 will help you. For the sample papers you can take as long as you need as you are learning and practising the process, but when you move on to the practice papers you should do them under exam conditions, taking 45 minutes for Level 1 papers and 1 hour for Level 2 papers, so that you can learn to work to time.

Practice

Sample papers with notes to help you are provided on pages 48–58, while further exam-style practice paper without notes given on pages 59–60.

Use the 'Top tips' on page 72 to help you complete the activities, to review your learning, and to revise before the tests.

Functional Skills
January 2008

000000
Level 1

ENGLISH
Writing
January 2008

AQA
ASSESSMENT AND
QUALIFICATIONS
ALLIANCE

Unit 0 000000 – Level 1

Make sure you have everything you need.

In addition to this paper you will require:
• An 8-page answer book

Specimen Paper

Time allowed: 45 minutes

Make a note of how long you have got – you need to allow time to answer all the questions.

Always read the instructions carefully.

Instructions

• Use blue or black ink or ball-point pen.
• Write the information required on the front of your answer book.
  The *Examining Body* for this paper is AQA.
• Answer question 1.
• Write your answer in the answer book provided.
• Do all your rough work in your answer book. Cross through any work
  you do not want to be marked.
• You may use a dictionary if you wish.

Do exactly what you are told to do – don't risk losing marks just because you haven't followed the instructions.

Make sure you have everything you need.

Information

• The maximum mark for this paper is 10.
• The marks for this question are shown in brackets.
• You are reminded of the need for good English and clear presentation
  in your answers. All questions should be answered in continuous prose.

Here is more useful information to help you do your best.

Advice

• You are advised to check your work carefully.

Always check your work and improve it if you can.

Sample Writing assessment Level 1

You will now practise working through the first four steps in a sample assessment before stopping to review in a Checkpoint.

1 Read the task

Task: Choose something you are interested in and know about. Write an informative article about your chosen subject for a magazine, website or newspaper of your choice.

Remember to:

- write to inform
- plan and organise what you are going to write
- use interesting words and sentences
- punctuate and spell accurately
- make sure your meaning is clear.

Before you begin writing, work through the next three steps.

2 Identify features of the task

The first thing you need to do is identify exactly what the task is. The easiest way to do this is to work out the **purpose** (what you have to do); the **audience** (who you are writing for); and the **form** (exactly what you are being asked to write). In this case:

PURPOSE: to inform readers about a subject of your choice
AUDIENCE: readers of your chosen magazine, website or newspaper
FORM: article.

3 Gather ideas

The next step is to gather ideas together. You need to have something to write about. Spend a few minutes jotting down things you could write about. Here is an example:

4 Organise your ideas

You need to present your ideas in a logical and ordered way. To do this you need to decide, in advance, the order in which you are going to give the detail to the reader. You may decide not to use some of your ideas.

Checkpoint

Before you move on to Step 5 and write your own article, you are going to assess the writing of another student. This will help you to identify good features of writing and focus on areas that need improvement. You should carry what you learn from this into your own writing.

a Read the example of a student's writing in response to the above task, at the top of page 49.
b List three things the student does well.
c List two things the student does not do well.
d Compare your ideas with another student's. Decide between you what this student should focus on in order to improve their writing.
e Set two targets for this student to improve their writing.

You are now ready to carry on with Steps 5 and 6 in the sample writing assessment.

Manchester United are one of the best football clubs in the world and I have supported them all my life.

Over the years Manchester United have been one of the best clubs around and in 1999 they won it all. Unite won the FA premier league, FA Cup and the hardest of them all the UEFA champions league. This was there greatest achivement under sir Alex and every Man United fan was prode.

Manchester United home shirt is red/white and there away shirt is white and gold. These t-shirts are worn all over the world in many different countries. It isn't just a football club anymore, it's a company. Fans were going mental when the club was bought out by some Americans for around £850 million.

Manchester United's home ground is Old Trafford and it is the biggest in All the English league's. When I go and watch united the noise that the fans make is unbelieveable and I always try and get behind my team.

The Red devels are the most successful English club just ahead of Liverpool and have won the league 15 times over the years. United are also the richest club in the world, until last year when Real Madrid just took over them.

Thire record signings are Wayne Rooney and Rio Ferdinand which both cost 30 million and there biggest win came at old Trafford in the premier league against Ipswich which ended 9-0 to united.

Manchester United's nick name is the red devils and they have a devil on their badge. Sir Alex Ferguson has been the manager for along time. He is one of the most successful managers ever and has won everything there is to win. There is much respect around Manchester United supporters and he has brought this succes to the club.

Man uniteds main rivals are Manchester city who only play down the road at the city of Manchester stadium. The fans love derby day but its not always that good for united fans as city have won a good few matches against them.

5 Write

Now write your own article. Your aim is to inform your reader in an interesting way.
Your writing should:

- be organised, detailed and clear
- be grammatically correct
- have accurate punctuation
- have accurate spelling
- have varied sentences and vocabulary.

6 Check, correct and improve your writing

Check your writing for spelling, punctuation and grammar. Is the meaning clear?
Is your writing effective and suitable for its audience and purpose?
Could you change some words or phrases to make it more effective?

Checkpoint

a Assess your own writing. Identify three things that you do well and two things that need improving.
b Set yourself two targets for improving your next piece of writing.

Sample Writing assessment Level 2

You will now practise working through the first four steps in another sample assessment before stopping to review in a Checkpoint.

1 Read the task

Write the text for an advert for a machine of your choice. Choose your target audience and inform them about the machine and persuade them to buy it. Remember to:

- write to inform *and* persuade
- plan and organise your response
- use a range of sentence structures and vocabulary
- paragraph appropriately
- check your work.

Before you begin writing, work through the next three steps.

2 Identify features of the task

The first thing you need to do is identify exactly what the task is. The easiest way to do this is to work out the **purpose** (what you have to do); the **audience** (who you are writing for); and the **form** (exactly what you are being asked to write). In this case, they are:

PURPOSE: to inform readers about the machine and persuade them to buy it
AUDIENCE: readers who might be interested in the machine
FORM: text for an advert

3 Gather your ideas

The next stage is to gather ideas together. You need to have something to write about. Spend a few minutes jotting down things you could write about. Here is an example:

4 Organise your ideas

You need to present your ideas in a logical and ordered way. To do this you need to decide, in advance, the order in which you are going to give the detail to the reader. You may decide not to use some of your ideas.

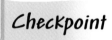

Checkpoint

Before you move on to Step 5 and write the text for your own advert, you are going to assess the writing of another student. This will help you to identify good features of writing and focus on areas that need improvement. You should carry what you learn from this into your own writing.

a Read the example of a student's writing in response to the above task, on page 51.
b List three things the student does well.
c List two things the student does not do well.
d Compare your ideas with another student's. Decide between you what this student should focus on in order to improve their writing.
e Set two targets for this student to improve their writing.

You are now ready to carry on with Steps 5 and 6 in the sample writing assessment.

Is it a bird? Is it a plane?

No! It's the new Lotus Supreme V8 Turbo and it's waiting for you to drive it away.

The new Lotus Supreme V8 Turbo comes in lots of different colours from fireball red to midnight blue. It comes with electric windows, power steering, 4 wheel drive and what we call "Lamborghini doors"! Kerpow!

The V8 is mainly controlled by its smart-card key. This is the key that starts the engine of the car, opens the boot, changes the cd's in the 10 disc player, converts the car between open and rag-top and opens the air pressurised scissor doors.

Too much to take in all at once? I'll make it easier:
The Lotus Supreme V8 turbo is the one for you!

It is not available in stores just yet but, with my help and the trusty internet, you young fellas could order this baby online right now. You might have to pay a bit extra to get it over from America but it'll be worth every penny for the heads you'll turn.

SuperCars 4 Cool Guys are giving readers the chance to get hold of these 400 bhp monsters with the IQ of Einstein. For just $250,000 you could be taking delivery any day now. Grab it now. Be the first. It'll cost more later.

Every young man in his prime should be cruising around in one of these to catch the lady's eye.

5 Write

Now write your advert. Your aim is to find an interesting way to inform your reader about your chosen machine and persuade them to buy it. Your writing should:

- be organised, clear and detailed
- be grammatically correct
- have accurate punctuation
- have accurate spelling
- have varied sentences and vocabulary
- inform and persuade your chosen audience.

6 Check, correct and improve your writing

Check your writing for spelling, punctuation and grammar. Is the meaning clear?
Is your writing effective and suitable for its audience and purpose?
Could you change some words or phrases to make it more effective?

Checkpoint

a Assess your own writing. Identify three things that you do well and two things that need improving.
b Set yourself two targets for improving your next piece of writing.

Sample Writing assessment Level 1

You will now practise a Level 1 Writing assessment by completing the following paper, using the six steps to help you to structure your writing. Complete the task, then look at the examples of students' work on pages 53 and 54. These have been annotated by an examiner. Use the examiner's comments to help you to assess your own writing against what is required at Level 1 – look again at the table on page 46 if you need a reminder. Identify:

- what you do well
- what needs improving.

WRITING

Answer Question 1.

1   You have been organising a fun run for a local leisure centre. Write a leaflet in which you inform people about the fun run and tell them about how they can join in.

Tell them about:
- where and when the fun run will take place
- how long the run is and the route it will take
- how they can register
- where and when they are to meet
- what facilities will be available for them.

Remember to:
- write to inform
- plan and organise what you are going to say
- make the event seem attractive
- interest your reader by the sentences you use and the words you choose
- punctuate accurately
- check your spelling.

(10 marks)

END OF QUESTION   © AQA

---

1   Read the task
Make sure you have read the *whole* task and are clear about what is required.

2   Identify features of the task
Work out:
- the purpose (what you have to do)
- the audience (who you are writing for)
- the form (exactly what you are being asked to write).

3   Gather ideas
Look again at the bullet points under 'Tell them about' in the question. Jot them down, then make some notes next to each about what you will say. You may like to put them into a spidergram or a list.

4   Organise your ideas
Decide which order your information is to go in. Number your points. Cross out anything you decide not to include but make sure you include everything listed in 'Tell them about'.

5   Write
Write your leaflet. Make sure you follow the bullet points listed under 'Remember to' in the question.

6   Check, correct and improve your writing
Is your writing clear and accurate? Use your dictionary to check your spelling. Make any changes you can to improve your writing. Have you included all the necessary information? Remember to cross out all your rough work and planning once you have completed the task.

Sample Writing assessment Level 1: work by Student A

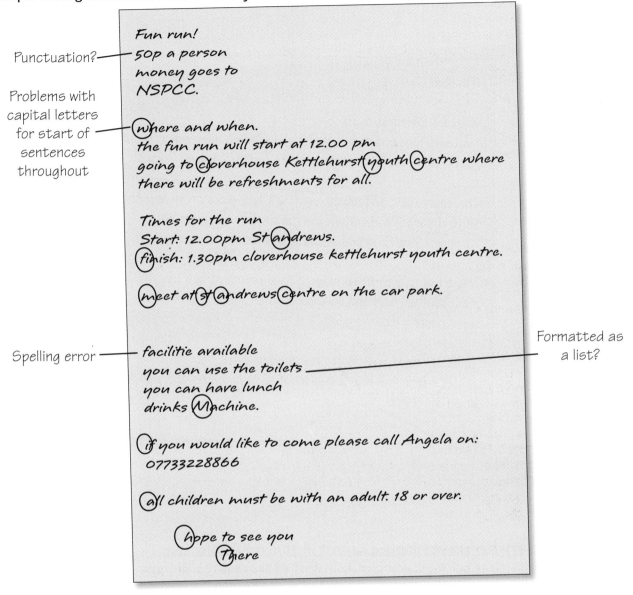

Punctuation?

Problems with capital letters for start of sentences throughout

Spelling error

Formatted as a list?

Fun run!
50p a person
money goes to
NSPCC.

where and when.
the fun run will start at 12.00 pm
going to cloverhouse Kettlehurst youth centre where
there will be refreshments for all.

Times for the run
Start: 12.00pm St andrews.
finish: 1.30pm cloverhouse kettlehurst youth centre.

meet at st andrews centre on the car park.

facilitie available
you can use the toilets
you can have lunch
drinks Machine.

if you would like to come please call Angela on:
07733228866

all children must be with an adult. 18 or over.

hope to see you
There

Examiner's summary of marking against what is required for Level 1
- The meaning is clear and coherent. There is some detail, although the student has forgotten to include the date, how long the run is, the route and how to register.
- The sequencing is logical.
- The language is appropriate and it is clearly structured. The format isn't suitable but would not need much correction.
- Most of the grammar is correct, although only some of it is in proper sentences.
- There are major problems with capital letters and only some sentences are correctly punctuated. It needs to be clearer what is intended to be in list form. The colon and exclamation mark are well used.

Overall: not quite a Level 1. The student needs to use capital letters correctly, make the sentences more accurate and include more of the required information.

Sample Writing assessment Level 1: work by Student B

Clear heading

Some careless errors

Unchecked — spelling errors

Phone number missing

Good choice of words

> Fun Run!
>
> Welcome Local residents.
> I'm David Ling and in this leaflet you will find information about
> A fun run I have been organising for our local leisure centre.
>
> This spectacular and unique event will take place on Wednesday
> 17th Febuary. The event will start at the leisure centre on
> Packhorse Road and end at Christie hospital, at Dagenham.
>
> It is a five mile route so I myself have estimated how long the fun
> run Event will take and have come to an agreement of
> three hours.
>
> There are three ways to register for this event. You can either:
> collect A form, fill it in and bring it back; go online and sign up,
> or on the phone

Examiner's summary of marking against what is required for Level 1
- This is clear, coherent and contains most of the required information. It lacks the starting time, facilities and phone number.
- The sequence is perfectly clear and logical.
- The format and structure are generally satisfactory. Language is effectively chosen to attract the readers' attention.
- The grammar is correct until the very end.
- Though there are punctuation errors and one spelling mistake, the meaning is clear throughout. The mistakes could probably have been avoided if the writing had been carefully checked.

Overall: this meets the requirements for Level 1.

Sample Writing assessment Level 2

You will now practise a Level 2 Writing assessment by completing the following paper, using the six steps to help you to structure your writing. Complete the task, then look at the examples of students' work on pages 56 and 57. These have been annotated by an examiner. Use the examiner's comments to help you to assess your own writing against what is required at Level 2 – look again at the table on page 46 if you need a reminder.
Identify: • what you do well • what needs improving.

WRITING

Answer Question 1.

1   You are organising a fundraising event for a charity.

Choose which charity you are raising money for and what kind of event you are organising.

Write an article for your local newspaper in which you persuade readers to attend the event.

Tell them about:
• where and when the event will take place
• what will happen at the event
• how they can get there.

Persuade them to attend:
• by what you choose to say
• by the language you use.

Remember to:
• write to persuade
• plan and organise what you are going to say
• make the event seem attractive
• use a range of appropriate sentences
• use appropriate sections or paragraphs
• check your work for accuracy and meaning.

(15 marks)

END OF QUESTION

---

1   **Read the task**
Make sure you have read the *whole* task and are clear about what is required.

2   **Identify features of the task**
Work out:
• the purpose (what you have to do)
• the audience (who you are writing for)
• form (exactly what you are being asked to write).

3   **Gather ideas**
Look again at the bullet points under 'Tell them about' and 'Persuade them to attend' in the question. Make notes about what you will say and the language you will use. You may like to put them into a spidergram or a list.

4   **Organise your ideas**
Order your information and ideas and number your points. Cross out any you decide not to include but make sure you include all the required information. Remember the form – what kind of layout should you use?

5   **Write**
Write your article. Make sure you follow the bullet points listed under 'Remember to' in the question.

6   **Check, correct and improve your writing**
Is your writing clear and accurate? Use your dictionary to check your spelling. Does it inform *and* persuade? Have you included all the necessary information? Make any changes you can to improve your writing. Remember to cross out all your rough work and planning once you have completed the task.

Sample Writing assessment Level 2: work by Student C

Headline missing

Persuasive language

Some accurate spelling of difficult words but some careless errors in spelling also

Information on start time and how to get there is missing

If you are interested in charity and want to raise money for people less fortunate than yourself? Then come along to the homeless charity event that will take place on the 1st March 2008 This event will be nothing like you have ever been, to before. It will be held at the Harlequin Centre. You will be asked to pay £1 per person to enter but it will be worth it.

This event will be fun for all the family. There will be some spectacular things to experience such as an auction where there will be 10 pairs of tickets to watch Arsenal going under the hammer. Also there will be bouncy castles, trampolines, buffet, fun fair (outside) and also a penalty shoot out against England Goalkeeper Paul Robinson. With a chance to win an LCD HD TV.

After that there will be a fun run where the person who completes an obsticle the fastest could win a trolley dash around the harlequin centre. For every person who participates in this challenge they will recieve a certificate. However you will be asked to pay £1.50 to enter this obstical course.

That's not all there will be an autograph signing with the England team. David Beckham, Wayne Rooney and Steven Gerrard are just some of the stars that are going to be there.

If this sounds like your cup of tea then come on down to the Harlequin Centre. For More information contact event Manager Peter Jones or email. Telephone 0723 4567890
Email: pjonescharity@hotmail.com

<u>Examiner's summary of marking against what is required for Level 2</u>

- There is appropriate information, though this student forgets to include the start time and how to get there. There are many attempts to persuade through the attractions described and the language chosen.
- The information is clear and concise as well as logically sequenced.
- The language is appropriate and it is clearly structured. The format is appropriate for a local newspaper article, although a headline would have been useful.
- There is a range and some variety of sentence structures.
- Punctuation is mainly accurate although there are errors. There is evidence of the correct use of each item of punctuation, despite the mistakes.
- The meaning is always clear. Errors tend to be small and not frequently repeated. A wide range of punctuation is accurately used, despite the missing full stop, errors in capital letters, and the odd question mark and comma. The grammar is accurate. Spelling is generally correct despite the two wrong versions of 'obstacle'.

Overall: despite the small technical errors, this meets all of the requirements for Level 2. It is a shame that the work was unchecked.

Sample Writing assessment Level 2: work by Student D

Interesting word choices

Headline missing

Good range of sentence structures

Two errors in spelling and punctuation

Good range of sentence structures

Is February getting you down? Are you at a loose end when it comes to weekend activities, and at a loss as to what to do with the kids? If so, energise yourself and your family with a trip to the British Heart Foundation's 'Heart Healthy' Family Fun Day, this year taking place on the 4th May, from 10:30 – 2:30, in Tiverton.

The event is now in its seventh year, having proved a fantastic success in recent years, raising a whopping £27,000 for the Foundation, whose vital work to combat heart disease relies on donations from the public. Last year, the British Heart Foundation was able to pay for over 200 CT scanners in hospitals across the UK, allowing heart disease, now considered an epidemic as a result of the sedentary Western lifestyle, to be detected at an early stage. Remember, heart disease is the UK's biggest killer. It can strike anyone – including you.

So, if you fancy helping this good cause, why not pop along to Tiverton Heath, right next to the railway station in the town centre, for 3 hours of fun and games for all the family (there is even a party lunch included FREE for children under 10!). Children, teeneagers, adults, grandparents: all will be catered for!

For the children, Mr Heart, the lovable rosy-red mascot for the BHF, will be there to entertain and educate your children about the importance of a healthy lifestyle. In addition, feel free to have a go on the bouncy castle; check out the face painting area; whiz around on the go-karts and quadbikes; or try your luck on Billy the Bucking Bronco!

For those whose childhood years have sadly passed them by, why not have a go on the tombola, meander through our vast selection of discount books, clothes and CDs; or watch the dazzling, hypnotic falconry and classic cars at the central arena? Fortunately, if you get a bit peckish, a variety of snacks, and drinks and cold buffet nibbles will be provided: all easy on your heart – and your wallet! Finally, the hypochondriacs among us may well be tempted by the free blood pressure testing kit; lets find out if you really are as healthy as you thought!

So there you have it – a day of joyful joviality for all concerned. We hope to see you there, 10:30-2:30, 4th May at Tiverton Heath, helping to raise money for a charity which really is a lifeline to so many. It is people like you who save lives, so make sure you don't miss out.

Interesting word choices

<u>Examiner's summary of marking against what is required for Level 2</u>

- This is clear, coherent and contains all the required information.
- The sequence is perfectly clear and logical.
- Despite the lack of a headline, the article is very well arranged and very well written, with language, sentence structures and information most effectively chosen to persuade.
- A wide range of sentence structures is employed most effectively.
- There is one missing apostrophe and one spelling mistake. Otherwise it is technically completely accurate. The meaning is clear throughout and often stylishly conveyed.

Overall: this meets the requirements for Level 2. It gains full marks, despite the absence of a headline and small technical errors.

Practice Writing assessment 1 Level 1

Practise a Level 1 Writing assessment by completing the following paper. You are reminded of the need for good English and clear presentation in your answer. The question should be answered in continuous prose. You are advised to check your work carefully. You may use a dictionary if you wish. You have 45 minutes to complete the paper.

WRITING

Answer Question 1.

1   Your local Water Board wants people to drink tap water instead of bottled water.

You have been asked to write a leaflet from the Water Board to householders, informing them about:
- the advantages of drinking tap water
- the problems with drinking bottled water.

Tell them about:
- what the tap water is like
- why they should drink it
- why they should not drink bottled water.

If you want to, you can include some of the following topics:

TASTE   HEALTH   AVAILABILITY

COST   POLLUTION   WASTE

Remember to:
- write to inform
- plan and organise what you are going to say
- write a leaflet
- interest your reader by the sentences you use and the words you choose
- punctuate accurately
- check your spelling.

(10 marks)

END OF QUESTION

© AQA

Practice Writing assessment 2 Level 1 and Level 2

Practise a Level 1 and Level 2 Writing assessment by completing the following paper. You are reminded of the need for good English and clear presentation in your answer. The question should be answered in continuous prose. You are advised to check your work carefully. You may use a dictionary if you wish. You have 1 hour to complete the paper.

WRITING

Answer Question 1.

1   Your local water board is running a campaign to try to get people to drink tap water instead of bottled water .

You have been asked to write a leaflet from the water board to householders persuading them to drink tap water.

Tell them about:
- the tap water you provide
- why they should drink it
- why they should not drink bottled water.

Persuade them:
- by what you choose to say
- by the language you use.

Remember to:
- plan and organise what you are going to say
- write to inform and persuade
- write a leaflet
- use a range of sentence structures
- check your punctuation and spelling
- check your work for accuracy and meaning.

(15 marks)

END OF QUESTION

© AQA

Unit 3 Speaking and Listening

Throughout your course, your teacher will assess your speaking and listening skills. You will take part in a range of activities and your teacher will choose the two in which you did best to award your final level. One of these will be a discussion and the other will be a presentation. You need to pass the discussion to achieve a Level 1, and the discussion *and* the presentation to achieve Level 2.

Use the 'Top tips' on page 74 to help you complete the activities, to renew your learning, and to revise before the tests.

Thinking about discussion

In its widest sense, the term discussion means the spoken exchange of information, ideas or opinions between two or more people.

The different levels

The following lists show you what you need to do for each level in a discussion.

Discussion Level 1

- Make relevant contributions to discussions, responding appropriately to others.
- Prepare for and contribute to formal discussion by thinking of ideas and opinions.
- Be flexible in discussion, making different kinds of contribution.
- Present information/points of view clearly and in appropriate language.

Discussion Level 2

- Listen to complex information and give a relevant, cogent response in appropriate language.
- Present information and ideas clearly and persuasively to others.
- Adapt contributions in discussions to suit audience, purpose and situation.
- Make significant contributions to discussions, taking a range of roles and helping to move the discussion forward to reach decisions.

Thinking about presentation

In a presentation the spotlight is very much on your individual performance. You may be working with other people but you will be assessed on how well you, as an individual, present your material to your audience.

The different levels

The following bullets show you what you need to do for each level in a presentation.

Presentation Level 1

- Present information/points of view clearly and in appropriate language.

Presentation Level 2

- Present information and ideas clearly and persuasively to others.

Sample Speaking and Listening assessment: Discussion

In this section you will prepare for and take part in a discussion by working through five steps:

- You will prepare for the discussion by reading the section 'Preparing for your discussion' below, and then following steps 1 and 2 on page 63 on your own.
- You will then work in a group of three or four and follow steps 3, 4 and 5 on page 63.

Your task is to establish, through discussion and negotiation, a set of five rules for group discussion that each member of your group will agree to follow.

Preparing for your discussion

Whether you are in a group of two or ten, it makes sense that you are all going to do your best work if the group works together. Below are some of the complaints often made by people taking part in group discussions. Read them and think about times when you, or students you know, may have felt the same way.

There's always one who just messes about and distracts everyone.

Nobody really listens to anyone else.

She makes a joke out of everything even when it's serious.

No one will ever make a decision.

We never manage to get the task finished on time.

You have to shout if you really want to be heard.

I always get the blame if something goes wrong.

There's a couple of people who do all the talking.

I never get the chance to say what I want to, when I want to.

Five steps for discussions

1 On your own, and using your experience of group discussions to help you, make two lists in a table like the one below:

Things I think *prevent* good group discussion	Things I think *help* good group discussion

2 Now think about the part you play in group discussion by answering the following questions honestly:

- Are you a good listener?
- Do you express your own ideas clearly and effectively?
- Do you help others to express their ideas?
- Do you make sure everyone is given the opportunity to speak?

Make a list of the things you could do better in order to help group discussion.

3 Now join your group. You have ten minutes in which to agree a set of five rules for group discussion. During those ten minutes you should make sure that:

- someone is making notes on what the group says – this does not have to be the same person the whole way through the discussion
- everyone has a chance to give their point of view
- all discussion is focused on the task
- there is discussion about which are the most important rules
- the five rules are agreed, and written down
- each person in the group agrees to follow the five rules.

4 At the end of the ten minutes, each group member should make a copy of the agreed rules. You will then disband and form new groups of three or four. You should not be working with anyone from your previous group.

5 Your task now is to conduct a second discussion. This is to agree between you a final set of rules by choosing the best ones from each person. To achieve the best you can you will need to:

- listen closely to what others say
- inform the group of your agreed rules clearly and explain the reasons for them
- be prepared to discuss, negotiate and compromise.

You have ten minutes in which to complete this task.

Checkpoint

You are going to assess how well you participated in the group discussions.

a Think back through the part you played in each of the two group discussions. Using the level guidance on page 61 to help you, decide which of the bullet points you achieved in Level 1 and/or Level 2.

b For each bullet you choose, write what you did to achieve it.

Sample Speaking and Listening assessment: Presentation

In this section you will prepare and deliver a presentation. This is similar to the type of task you may be asked to complete for your assessment.

Your task is to prepare and present a talk on a subject you feel strongly about. It could be about music, travel, cinema, sport, politics, religion – anything about which you have strong feelings and enough information. Your talk should be between three and five minutes long. Your aims are to:

- present your information and ideas clearly
- use appropriate language
- present your information and ideas persuasively.

The key to a successful presentation is in the preparation. Follow these steps:

1 **Choose your subject carefully:** It is important to choose a subject that you will be able to talk about in an interesting way. If you are not interested in it, it's unlikely you will be able to make your listeners interested in it. Try not to make your subject too broad. For example, it's usually more effective to talk about one kind of music than music in general.

2 **Make notes:** Jot down anything you can think of relating to your chosen subject. If you can't think of many things, you haven't chosen the right subject. You may need to do some extra research on certain details in your notes. Use the internet and the library to help you.

3 **Select material:** You don't need to tell your listeners everything you know about your chosen subject. Pick out from your notes the details that are most likely to interest them. These are the things you should concentrate on in your talk.

4 **Decide on the best order:** You know about your chosen subject. Your listeners may not. You need to choose the best order in which to present the information to them. Make sure you think about how each point can be linked to the next one.

5 **Give examples:** Real-life examples or anecdotes (brief real-life experiences) can make a talk more interesting and persuasive. Decide on one or two of these that you could include in your talk.

6 **Use prompt cards:** Once you have decided on the content and order of your talk, you could create prompt cards. These are designed to help you keep track of what you want to say and not miss out anything important. Remember, you cannot read out a presentation. Your prompt cards should only contain brief notes.

7 **Use support materials:** This is optional. A talk can be made more interesting by the use of a few support materials such as photographs or other visual images. Avoid passing these round during your talk, however, as they simply distract your audience from what you are saying.

8 **Practise:** Your talk should last between three and five minutes. Less than that and you have not prepared enough material – more, and you are in danger of boring your audience. Go through what you want to say several times, making sure the words you choose are clear and your talk is well timed.

9 **Use your voice:** We all know how boring it can be to listen to someone who never changes their tone of voice. Think about how you will say the things you want to and where you should pause for maximum effect.

10 **Remember body language:** It doesn't matter how interesting the content of your talk is, if you do not address your listeners directly and mumble at the floor, they will be bored. Look at your listeners, make eye contact and they will listen. If you get the chance, practise in front of a friend and ask them to give you feedback on your body language.

11 **Be confident:** You've done your preparation well. You've practised your talk. Decide now that you are not going to let nerves get the better of you. Take a deep breath, smile and begin.

12 **Invite questions:** At the end of your talk, ask if there are any questions. Listen to these carefully and answer them clearly and, where appropriate, in detail.

Checkpoint

a Ask four of your listeners to copy and complete the following feedback form and assess your own performance.

	Yes	No
Did the speaker make a range of different points?	☐	☐
Did you learn new things about the chosen subject?	☐	☐
Were the points clearly linked to each other?	☐	☐
Did the speaker give interesting examples?	☐	☐
Did the speaker make good use of prompt cards?	☐	☐
Were support materials used to make the talk more interesting?	☐	☐
Did the talk last between three and five minutes?	☐	☐
Did the speaker vary the tone of his/her voice?	☐	☐
Did the speaker make eye contact with the listeners?	☐	☐
Did the speaker answer any questions clearly and in an appropriate amount of detail?	☐	☐

Write one thing that the speaker could have done to make the talk more effective:

_____

b Based on the feedback, set three targets for yourself that will help you to do even better next time.

Practice Speaking and Listening assessments: Discussion

Before tackling each of these assignments, turn to page 61 and remind yourself of:

- what you need to do to meet the criteria for Level 1 and Level 2 in discussions
- the things that help good group discussions.

Assessment 1

Your school or college has been awarded a grant of £10,000 to improve the working environment for students. In pairs or groups of three, discuss how this money could be best spent either on a single thing or on a range of things. Use the following prompts to help you structure and develop your discussion. The whole task should take 25 to 30 minutes.

- Spend between 5 and 10 minutes talking about different ways the money could be used to improve the working environment for students. Take time to explore different options and points of view.

You now have 15 minutes to complete the task.

- Make a list of all the suggestions made and the ways in which each of these would improve the working environment for students.
- Agree a priority order for the suggestions made.
- Make realistic estimates of the cost of each one. Check on the internet or with your teacher if you are not sure.
- Decide on your final recommendations.

Checkpoint

You are going to assess how well you participated in this group discussion.

- Using the level guidance on page 61 to help you, decide which of the bullet points you achieved in Level 1 and/or Level 2.
- For each bullet you choose, write down what you did to achieve it.
- Set yourself one target for improving your performance in your next group discussion. Write it down.

Assessment 2

Your teacher has offered to arrange a day out for your class or group as a reward for 100% attendance, providing that you can all agree a destination and itinerary for the day. Your task is to agree a destination and provide a detailed outline of the day. If you want to, you can stop at other places on the way there or back. Work in groups of three. Use the following prompts to help you to structure and develop your discussion.

- Spend between 5 and 10 minutes talking about possible destinations, taking into account individual preferences, distances and potential costs.

You now have 15 minutes to complete the task.

- Select the two most popular choices. List the points in favour of and against each of these.
- Use your list of points in favour and against to help you make your final choice and then agree a detailed outline for the day. This should include: departure and arrival times; transport arrangements; a range of activities for the day; possible additional stop-off points and suggestions for where and when to eat.
- Consider and agree ways of making your chosen destination appear the most attractive of the possible choices if it were put to a class vote.

Checkpoint

You are going to assess how well you participated in this group discussion.
- Using the level guidance on page 61 to help you, decide which of the bullet points you achieved in Level 1 and/or Level 2.
- For each bullet you choose, write down what you did to achieve it.
- Set yourself one target for improving your performance in your next group discussion. Write it down.

Assessment 3

In groups of three or four, choose <u>one</u> of the following questions about which you have a range of views:

> Should uniform be compulsory in a place of study or work?
>
> Should the use of mobile phones be allowed in a place of study or work?
>
> Should the age for obtaining a full driving licence be raised to 20?

Use the following prompts to help you structure and develop your discussion.

- Spend a few minutes on your own thinking about the chosen question and jotting down possible points that would support a 'Yes' answer and possible points that would support a 'No' answer.

- In your group, make a chart with two columns, like the one below. Spend about five minutes discussing the points that could be entered in each column. Where there is general agreement, write these points down. Aim to have at least four clear points in each column.

Should uniform be compulsory in a place of study or work?	
Yes	No

- Once the chart is completed, take it in turns to give your personal response to the question, having carefully considered the range of points that have been made by other students.

- When you have given your view and listened to the points of other students you need to decide on a definite answer to the question. Each member of the group should register a 'Yes' or 'No' vote. The decision of the majority (the most members of the group) should be taken as the final answer. Where there is a draw (equal numbers for and against) no final answer can be given. If this happens, you could review all the points made to see if anyone wants to change their vote.

Checkpoint

You are going to assess how well you participated in this group discussion.
- Using the level guidance on page 61 to help you, decide which of the bullet points you achieved in Level 1 and/or Level 2.
- For each bullet you choose, write down what you did to achieve it.
- Write a report on your current performance in group discussion. Your report should be between 50 and 100 words.
- Use any weaknesses you identify to set yourself a target for improving your performance in your next group discussion.

Practice Speaking and Listening assessments: Presentation

Before tackling each of these assessments, turn to page 61 and remind yourself of what you need to do to meet the criteria for Level 1 and Level 2 in Presentation.

Assessment 1

Use the discussion Assessment 1 on page 66 as the basis for an individual or paired presentation to the governors of your school or college. If you have not completed this assessment, take ten minutes to consider the following:

Your school or college has been awarded a grant of £10,000 to improve the working environment for students. Decide how you think this money could be best spent, either on a single thing or on a range of things.

Your aim is to:

- present your point of view clearly in appropriate language
- persuade the governors to adopt your ideas.

Use the following prompts to help you structure and develop your presentation.

- Remind yourself of the points made in the discussion and of the conclusions your group made, or of your own decision on how the money could best be spent.
- Think about how to start your presentation. You could, for example, describe the current working environment for students or use photographs to illustrate it. This could be particularly effective if done as a PowerPoint presentation.
- Decide on the appropriate order in which to present your ideas to the governors. If you are making a combination of suggestions you may, for example, need to decide whether to start with the cheapest or most expensive one. Are there any obvious links between the suggestions that you could exploit? If you are making a single suggestion you will need to gather a range of reasons to justify your choice.
- Think about how to express your point of view clearly, using visual aids where appropriate. For example, a simple money chart indicates how the figures add up.
- Think about how to express your ideas persuasively. You need to engage your listeners through your tone, pacing and body language as well as through content.
- Take time to practise before making your final presentation.

Checkpoint

a Make your presentation to a group of students. Ask them to copy and complete the following feedback form. Make your own assessment of your performance too.

Did the speaker make a range of different points?	Yes ☐	No ☐
Did you learn new things about the chosen subject?	Yes ☐	No ☐
Were the points clearly linked to each other?	Yes ☐	No ☐
Did the speaker give interesting examples?	Yes ☐	No ☐
Did the speaker make good use of prompt cards?	Yes ☐	No ☐
Were support materials used to make the talk more interesting?	Yes ☐	No ☐
Did the talk last between 3 and 5 minutes?	Yes ☐	No ☐
Did the speaker vary the tone of his/her voice?	Yes ☐	No ☐
Did the speaker make eye contact with the listeners?	Yes ☐	No ☐

Write one thing that the speaker could have done to make the talk more effective:

_____

_____

b Based on the feedback and your own assessment, set one target for yourself that will help you to do better next time.

Use the following prompts to help you to prepare, structure and develop your presentation:

- Make a list of the points you would need to include in your explanation. Consider the needs of your audience – remember they know nothing about your chosen subject.
- Decide on the best order for coverage of these points so that you do not confuse your audience.
- Consider using visual aids to help your explanation. For example, a talk on how to play the guitar might be made more interesting if the audience could actually see it and hear you play. Similarly, a flow chart could help to clarify an explanation of how to make or do something.
- Think about how to express your ideas persuasively. You need to engage your listeners through your tone, pacing and body language as well as through content. If you want them to try it, you will need to sound enthusiastic.
- Take time to practise before making your final presentation.

Use the feedback format given on page 71 to help you assess your performance.

Assessment 2

This is an individual presentation based on explaining how to do something and persuading the listeners to have a go. Below are some suggestions for the type of thing you could choose.

- How to play a particular game or instrument.
- How to develop skills in a particular sport.
- How to make something.
- How to carry out a specific task, such as booking a holiday online.
- How to get a job.

You should assume that your audience has no knowledge of your chosen subject. Your aim is to:

- give a clear explanation in appropriate language
- persuade your listeners to have a go at it
- talk for between 3 and 5 minutes.

Checkpoint

a Give your presentation to a group of students. Ask them to copy and complete the following feedback form. Make your own assessment of your performance too.

Did the speaker make a range of different points?	Yes ☐	No ☐
Did you learn new things about the chosen subject?	Yes ☐	No ☐
Were the points clearly linked to each other?	Yes ☐	No ☐
Did the speaker give interesting examples?	Yes ☐	No ☐
Did the speaker make good use of prompt cards?	Yes ☐	No ☐
Were support materials used to make the talk more interesting?	Yes ☐	No ☐
Did the talk last between three and five minutes?	Yes ☐	No ☐
Did the speaker vary the tone of his/her voice?	Yes ☐	No ☐
Did the speaker make eye contact with the listeners?	Yes ☐	No ☐

Write one thing that the speaker could have done to make the talk more effective:

_____

b Based on the feedback and your own assessment, write a report on your current performance in presentation. Your report should be between 50 and 100 words. Include a target for improving your performance next time.

Top tips

Remembering ten key points for each of your three Functional English assessments will help you to focus on what is really important. Read and remember these 'top tips' for your reading, writing and speaking and listening assessments. Make sure you follow these tips to give yourself the best possible chance of success in Functional English.

Reading test

Before answering the questions:

1 Read the instructions on the front of the question paper carefully and follow them exactly.

2 Read the source texts closely, identifying the main points and ideas, before answering the questions on them.

When answering the questions:

3 Remember, the answer is based directly and only on the text/s and there is only one correct choice for each question. Read each question and each answer option carefully.

4 Eliminate the obviously wrong answers first when making your choices.

5 Remind yourself of the content of *both* texts, before answering the comparative questions.

6 Use some time at the end of the test to check your choices carefully.

Your answers should show that you can:

7 Read closely or scan the text to obtain the information you need – look out for headings and key words that might help you to find the part of the text you need for each question.

8 Identify the purpose of the text by thinking about *why* the writer wrote it. Then consider how the writer conveys his facts and opinions in the text through words and presentational features.

9 Think about what is being conveyed directly by the words and the presentational features and, for Level 2 tests, what might also be implied and suggested.

10 Identify what action, if any, the writer hopes the reader will take after reading the text.

Writing test

Before writing:

1 Read the instructions on the front of the question paper carefully and follow them exactly.

2 Read the task carefully and highlight key words to help you identify the purpose (what you have to do), the audience (who you are writing for) and the form (exactly what you are being asked to write, such as a letter, or an article) to help you gather a range of ideas.

3 Make a spidergram or a list of information and ideas.

4 Decide on the best order for the points you want to make. Number them in order and cross out anything you decide not to include.

When writing:

5 Make sure your writing is clear, coherent and appropriately developed. For example, how much detail do you need to include?

6 If the tasks ask you to, make sure you are persuasive in the way you use words and address your audience.

7 Make sure your writing is appropriate to your purpose and audience and is in the right form, for example a letter.

8 Aim to use a range of sentence structures and words, including technical vocabulary if necessary.

After writing:

9 Check your writing closely. Read it 'aloud' in your head. Use your dictionary to check your spelling, and correct any errors you spot in punctuation or grammar. Make any other changes that would improve your writing, watching out for any common errors you tend to make.

10 Remember to cross out all your rough work and planning once you have completed the task.

Speaking and Listening assessment

In all speaking and listening assessments:

1 Always prepare carefully and, where appropriate, make notes to help you.

2 Speak clearly to be heard and understood. Aim to engage and persuade your listeners through your tone, pacing and body language as well as through content.

3 Adapt what you say to suit your audience, purpose and situation, using formal and informal language appropriately.

4 Develop your ideas and opinions in detail, using examples to support what you say and showing you have considered other people's perspectives.

In discussions:

5 Be prepared both to contribute yourself and to allow others the opportunity to speak. Listen carefully and respond appropriately to what they say.

6 Ask and respond to questions appropriately, making sure you have understood the points made by others.

7 Be flexible and prepared to shift your viewpoint in order to reach good decisions.

In presentations:

8 Cover the points you want to make in a logical order, presenting your information and ideas clearly and persuasively.

9 Consider using visual aids and prompt cards, but never read directly from prepared notes.

10 Take time to practise a presentation in front of other students and learn from the feedback they give you.

Answers

Sample Reading assessment Level 1

Source A: 'One day she'll make you proud'

Source	Level	Question	Answer
A	1	1	C
A	1	2	C
A	1	3	A
A	1	4	D
A	1	5	D
A	1	6	D
A	1	7	C
A	1	8	A

Sample Reading assessment Level 2

Source B: 'The children who don't exist'

Source A and Source B

Source	Level	Question	Answer
B	2	9	C
B	2	10	B
B	2	11	A
B	2	12	D
B	2	13	A
A/B	2	14	A
A/B	2	15	C

Practice Reading assessment 1 Level 1

Source A: 'Give the gift of life'

Source B: 'Checking a plug'

Source	Level	Question	Answer
A	1	1	C
A	1	2	B
A	1	3	D
A	1	4	B
A	1	5	C
A	1	6	A
B	1	7	A
B	1	8	D
B	1	9	B
B	1	10	B
B	1	11	C
B	1	12	C

Practice Reading assessment 2 Level 1

Source A: 'Cyprotel Poseidonia Beach Hotel'

Source B: 'A Family Day Out to Remember'

Source	Level	Question	Answer
A	1	1	B
A	1	2	D
A	1	3	B
A	1	4	A
A	1	5	D
A	1	6	C
B	1	7	D
B	1	8	A
B	1	9	B
B	1	10	B
B	1	11	A
B	1	12	A

Practice Reading assessment 3 Level 1 and Level 2

Source A: 'do something!'

Source B:
'Motoring: Practical test for cars explained'

Source C: 'London Calling'

Source D: National Trust letter

Source C and Source D

Source E: 'How Long Are You Here For?'

Source F: 'Work & Study'

Source E and Source F

Source	Level	Question	Answer
A	1	1	C
A	1	2	B
A	1	3	D
A	1	4	B
A	1	5	C
A	1	6	A
B	1	7	C
B	1	8	D
B	1	9	D
B	1	10	A
B	1	11	B
B	1	12	C
C	2	13	D
C	2	14	A
C	2	15	B
C	2	16	D
C	2	17	C
D	2	18	A
D	2	19	C
D	2	20	D
D	2	21	C
D	2	22	B
C/D	2	23	A
C/D	2	24	D
E	2	25	C
E	2	26	A
E	2	27	B
E	2	28	D
E	2	29	D
F	2	30	C
F	2	31	A
F	2	32	D
F	2	33	A
F	2	34	C
E/F	2	35	B
E/F	2	36	D

AQA FUNCTIONAL ENGLISH

Practice Reading assessment 4 Level 1 and Level 2

Source A: 'Go Further'

Source B: 'Zoo Keeper'

Source C: What are Discovery Visits?

Source D: 'a cleaner, greener place to be'

Source C and Source D

Source E: Page from theatre brochure

Source F: Scotts of Stow cafetière

Source E and Source F

Source	Level	Question	Answer
A	1	1	C
A	1	2	D
A	1	3	B
A	1	4	C
A	1	5	B
A	1	6	A
B	1	7	B
B	1	8	C
B	1	9	D
B	1	10	B
B	1	11	A
B	1	12	C
C	2	13	C
C	2	14	B
C	2	15	B
C	2	16	D
C	2	17	C
D	2	18	C
D	2	19	D
D	2	20	C
D	2	21	B
D	2	22	B
C/D	2	23	B
C/D	2	24	A
E	2	25	C
E	2	26	D
E	2	27	A
E	2	28	D
E	2	29	B
F	2	30	A
F	2	31	D
F	2	32	B
F	2	33	D
F	2	34	C
E/F	2	35	A
E/F	2	36	B